LOST AND FOUND ALONG THE WAY

The Co-dependent Christian

BY THEODORE A. ZAWISTOWSKI, M.A., C.C.D.C.

FAIRWAY PRESS
Lima, Ohio

LOST AND FOUND ALONG THE WAY:
THE CO-DEPENDENT CHRISTIAN
(OLD VALUES FOR A NEW ERA)

FIRST EDITION
Copyright © 1992 by
Theodore A. Zawistowski

Scripture taken from the *New American Standard Bible* © 1960, 1962, 1963, 1968, 1971, 1972, 1973, 1975, 1977 by The Lockman Foundation. Used by permission.

If you have any information regarding material used in this book for which citations are unknown, please notify the Author so that future editions may accurately cite these sources.

7956 / ISBN 1-55673-533-2 PRINTED IN U.S.A.

Dedication

To my God, through His Spirit, who inspired me and directed me to write this book as part of His call to me . . .

To His Son Jesus and His Mother Mary for their love . . .

To me, who took up the challenge, forgave myself for my past, love myself today and continue to work on being the best me that I can be . . .

To my wife Marge, friends Joe, Linda, Paulette, and Fr. Ted, who have loved me, taught me, encouraged me and supported me . . .

To my sister, brothers, stepdaughters and others in my family, so they can know more of who I am . . .

To my parents, who did the best they could with what they had . . .

A special "thank you" to my editor, Linda Koco, for her time, expertise and encouragement, to Father Al Laubenthal for his theological and Scriptural help, and to Chuck Grabowski for his word processing/computer assistance.

Table Of Contents

Preface

What does it mean to be in recovery? First, an awareness that present behaviors and possibly some relationships are not life-giving; secondly, a belief in yourself — that you can change; and, thirdly, taking action to allow the recovery process to begin.

As you begin to work your recovery, change your behaviors, get healthier and feel more "whole," rather than fragmented, your life will *begin*. You will come *alive*! And with your new beginnings will come new found freedom — freedom to be the special, gifted, spectacular, rainbow-colored person that you are!

As your awareness becomes more acute, it might be necessary for you to receive individual counseling, treatment of addictive behavior, attend self-help groups and become educated about co-dependency and recovery skills and techniques. This book falls into the latter category.

This self-help book tells you immediately that you are not alone. The author, along with many others, walk the journey with you. Within these pages you may soon see yourself and, perhaps, feel lost. But keep reading, reflecting on your life experiences, praying and practicing your new behaviors. With the use of this handy guide, you will experience yourself as someone different — stronger, more independent with greater self-confidence, more self-assurance, more freedom, more centered and more whole. The **new you**!

Recovery takes time. Recovery takes courage and patience. It is so worth it. Not only will you have found your way, you will have found new life! Take the risk and get well! ". . . I came that they might have life and have it to the full (John 10:10)."

Paulette Snyder, O.S.U.
Cleveland, Ohio

Foreword

When I first saw the personality characteristics list of an Adult Child of an Alcoholic several years ago, I was baffled, mystified and amazed. After all, there were no alcoholics in my immediate family other than one uncle and my paternal grandfather. But they were not much of an influence on me and were more on an outer circle of my immediate family. But even so, how did "they," these people who compiled this list, how did "they" know so much about *me*? It was almost as if they had been observing me over the years and taking notes! This was something that puzzled as well as scared me.

Over the last few years two things were happening. One was that I personally was trying to make sense out of this information, but for a long time it seemed like I was trying to put a round peg in a square hole — it just didn't fit. The other was that the field of chemical dependency/co-dependency/human behavior began to determine that this characteristics list applied not only to Adult Children of Alcoholics, but also to children/individuals who had grown up in any number of different Dysfunctional Families: that included physical or sexual abuse, verbal abuse, workaholism, chronic illness, food addiction, gambling addiction, emotional neglect, post-traumatic stress, religious fanatiscism, etc. to name a few. I don't know exactly when these two elements intersected but when they did, things started to make sense.

I didn't write this book to vent my anger with my parents or my teachers or my Church. I didn't write this book because I'm looking for someone to blame. I wrote it to help me understand my roots as a way of helping me understand my present and to transcend that. And, hopefully sharing my journey will help others on theirs.

Crudely put, I believe that "you can't give what you ain't got." My parents were second generation Americans who were workaholics and task oriented. They did not take care of themselves. (I believe that abuse of one's self is learned behavior and is taught by one generation to another.) My mother has been ill ever since I can remember and nothing I could ever do could change that. I feel that my parents neglected me emotionally and did not know how to show affection or understanding. They were not good listeners. They did not take the time to listen. They were rigid, strict and angry people because they were overworked, tired and frustrated, and wondering how they were going to "make ends meet." When I look back on their lives and how they were robbed of their childhoods in their own families and their own circumstances, I *can* understand. I *do* understand. But, there is hurt. But, there is sorrow. But, there is anger. And, there is love . . . .

In my married life with my wife and my four grown stepdaughters, I have regrets. I have made mistakes, too. If I knew then what I know now, . . . maybe things could have been different, better. I think I made some improvements on my own upbringing, but try as I might, like the lyrics by Harry Chapin in the song "The Cat's in the Cradle," "my boy was just like me" — I was and am my parents' son. Some of the very same things that I dislike about how I was raised by my parents, some of the very same things that I told myself I would never do, I have done. Consciously or unconsciously, I can see them now with masterful hindsight. But this is not new. It highlights the human, Christian struggle. St. Paul talks about it in his epistle to the Romans: "I cannot even understand my own actions. I do not do what I want to do but what I hate. . . . I know that no good dwells in me, that is, in my flesh; the desire to do right is there, but not the power. What happens is that I do, not the good I will to do, but the evil I do not intend." (Romans 7:15/18-19)

Although I am making changes and growing and struggling with my recovery insights, it is also the reason that I cannot "cast the first stone" at my parents or anyone else for that matter. My hope is that through this redemptive process I will achieve a better understanding of myself, my brothers and sisters, and my God; and most importantly, that I can be me, because that is my personal route to salvation.

This book is an opportunity for Christians who feel empty, victimized, defeated, unhappy and frustrated to shed some new light on their situations and to learn something about co-dependency. In this process they may find that co-dependency is part of their problem, and that understanding more about this issue can bring them to a more fulfilling Christian life.

On the other hand, this book is an opportunity for codependents who are in recovery and who were raised as Christians to see that a more accurate perspective on their Christian faith can lead to a harmony between their faith and their recovery process. They do not have to give up their Christianity in order to deal with their co-dependency.

The book moves from a "lost non-recovering, co-dependent Christian" to a "found recovering, co-dependent Christian." This progression from being "lost" to being "found" is not to be taken lightly. As Father John Loya tells us, for the Christian, "To be lost is to be dead; to be found is to be brought back to life."[1] Interestingly this is also the case with the journey of co-dependency recovery. It is this dual journey that will be chronicled in this book.

Introduction

I don't remember where I got it, but the poster was important to me as a teenager growing up. I kept it until my early years of college, but then, dirty and tattered, I threw it away. It pictured a girl, twelvish, running in a meadow with beautiful wildflowers surrounding her up to her waist. She was smiling with delight as the sun glistened off her long blonde hair. The caption read, ''Don't run, go slowly, for it's only to yourself that you have to go.'' Striving to live the meaning of those words seemed to slip away when I discarded the poster. But I rediscovered the words and the meaning some twenty years later as I embarked on my journey of co-dependency recovery.

As I look back on my life from the perspective of "middle age," I see a shy, introspective, often scrupulous, teenager who kept thoughts and feelings "bottled up" inside so they wouldn't "get out" and embarrass him. He needed to have rigid control of these thoughts and feelings, because they could be sinful. He wanted to be a good Catholic, a good son, a good boy, a good person. It was better to keep the thoughts and feelings inside than to risk letting them out and not know what might happen. It became increasingly important to please others, to take care of them, to be helpful, to be liked, to be good.

I learned at my mother's knee and at my father's side to be dependent on what others thought or felt for my sense of self worth. I learned to be a workaholic — that I *am* what I *do*, and that the more I do, the better I am. Time spent on myself was wasted, unproductive, selfish, bordering on sinful. I learned to be a martyr and to strive for perfection, though never achieving it. I learned to be co-dependent.

But I also learned to be Christian. I learned the value of prayer, respect, concern for others, and spiritual values. I learned that helping other people made me happy. This seemed to be what Christianity was all about. And that was part of the enigma. What better way to serve God, please my family, take care of others, and save my soul, than to be a priest? It seemed like the best of all possible worlds. So, mentally and emotionally, I started grooming myself for the priesthood at an early age.

My idols were the priests and nuns at school and church. I would pretend that I said mass, using Necco wafers as hosts. I wanted to be good. I became scrupulous and tried to suppress "impure thoughts." In eighth grade, when I won a week at Camp Notre Dame for the summer by writing an article on vocations, I wanted to give it away because some other boy probably deserved it more than I did. Besides, I was too shy to go to a strange place and be away from the security of home for a whole week. (Fortunately Father Joe persuaded me that it was OK for me to go.)

I remember anger as being the predominant feeling in my family as I was growing up. (This seemed rather contradictory to our Christian beliefs.) It also seemed to be OK to express anger within the family but not to outsiders, because then they wouldn't like us. I had developed a "bad temper" myself. As I got into my teens, I remember thinking that I did not want to be "like that," and also, that as a Christian, this was wrong. But along with anger, most of my other feelings became repressed, too.

I learned to avoid feeling by doing, by keeping busy, by feeding my workaholism. I also learned avoidance of feelings by worrying, making mental and written lists, and recycling compulsive thoughts. This enabled me to have some control over my thoughts, but not my feelings. I found myself in a vicious cycle.

With all this going on inside, I still drew my positive strokes from other people. I had become a good "people pleaser" and caretaker. And I was also trying to be a good Christian.

Wha does it mean to be a Christian? I do not intend for this book to be a theological treatise. For me, simply put, to be Christian is to acknowledge Jesus Christ as my Lord and

Savior and to try to live my life in accordance with that belief. I believe that my life is to be one of service to others and love of God. Of course this is much easier written than done!

What does it mean to be co-dependent? The popularity of this term has grown so there are many ways of describing it. One is "Saying 'yes' when you mean 'no.' " For example, something really makes you angry, but rather than express your true feeling, you brush it off and say something like, "Oh that's OK, no problem!" Of course this is a pattern of response, not an isolated incident. That's what makes it a problem for someone.

Another view is that co-dependency is an unhealthy focus outside the self. Melody Beattie, author of *CoDependent No More*, defines a co-dependent as "a person who has let someone else's behavior affect him or her and is obsessed with controlling other people's behavior."[1] Another definition is "Co-dependency is 'a psychosocial condition that is manifested through a dysfunctional pattern of relating to others.' This pattern is characterized by extreme focus outside of self, lack of open expression of feelings, and attempts to derive a sense of purpose through relationships with others."[2] Another "rule of thumb" definition is that co-dependency occurs when helping you hurts me. (For further characteristics and co-dependent patterns of behavior, refer to Appendix I.)

But this is not a treatise on co-dependency either. Rather it is a story of someone who is both Christian *and* co-dependent. When I began again that elusive journey into self that my poster talked about I found myself in a co-dependency recovery group. What I learned about myself left me no doubt that just as much as I believed my faith to be Christian, so also was my behavior co-dependent.

What I began to discover seemed shocking. As I started to learn about co-dependency and co-dependency recovery, it seemed like many of the recommended activities and thoughts and expressions were, well, self-centered. They also seemed to be self*ish*. (Exactly what I needed to balance with other-centeredness that had ruled my life.) But it was all so new, this business of "taking care of *me*." It took some getting used to. And then it started to feel un-Christian! Could it be that what I needed to do to become emotionally more healthy was placing my Christian values in jeopardy? After all, this talk about "me, myself and I" (the un-holy trinity from my childhood) was what I was taught to be prideful and sinful. And to add more strain, it appeared that besides my parents, my religion had contributed to my being co-dependent!

Was my Christianity part of the problem, rather than part of the solution? Would I ever be able to love again? Did I really know what love was? What had I gotten into? Change is hard. I didn't want to feel worse, I wanted to feel better! For God's sake, Lord, help me!!

He did. I began to see that for a co-dependent person like me, Christian principles as reinforced by religion and the institutional Church helped to perpetuate co-dependency. Of course recovery is based on a spiritual dimension, and for me, in this context, "spiritual" equals "Christian." So the emphasis and misinterpretation of Christian principles needs to be re-stated to aid in the recovery process. Christianity is not incompatible with recovery, but needs re-evaluation. Rather than being opposed or contradictory, Christianity and co-dependency recovery have the same goal. As the Army ad said, "Be all that you can be!"

I saw that God the Father, His Son, Jesus Christ, and the Spirit were my Higher Power (that's self-help lingo for "God as we understood Him" — some people choose nature or their recovery group, etc.) and that I did not need to "start from scratch" or come up with something chic or novel.

I never really felt that I had given up my Christian values, but as I began to experience self-affirmation, expression of feelings, assertiveness, not "caretaking" others, setting boundaries, not accepting others' responsibilities, loving myself and other recovery principles, many of these dynamics seemed contrary to how I was raised in my family, in Catholic school and in Church. I was working against some forty years of experience. Were recovery and my faith incompatible? Did I have to chose one or the other? I came to realize that the answer was, "No." In reality, for me, the two have a symbiotic relationship.

The process for me has been like going on a retreat or a sabbatical of self-love and self-exploration, if you will; to really get to know, understand, accept and appreciate myself. But not to remain focused inward, but rather, empowered by the Spirit, to truly believe and understand the miracle that I am and then to give that miracle back to God's service — ". . . . the man who has faith in me will do the works I do, and greater far than these." (John 14:12)

What is co-dependency? Are you co-dependent?

What is Christianity? Are you Christian?

If you answered "yes" to both sets of questions, which came first?

Is co-dependency just a "catch-all" phrase for "growing up?"

Has co-dependency had any impact on your life?

(Refer to Appendix I for Co-Dependency Characteristics List) Which of these can you identify with? Give some examples of "people pleasing" and controlling/manipulating on your part.

Do you feel guilty when you take time for yourself? If so, why? What other situations or circumstances occasion guilt in you?

Have you experienced any of this conflict between taking care of yourself — being "selfish" — and your Christian, other-centered upbringing?

How have you attempted to resolve this conflict?

CHAPTER I
Ten "Old" Mandates From Scripture

O God, Our Help In Ages Past

*O God, our Help in ages past, Our
Hope for years to come. Our Shelter from the
stormy blast, And our eternal Home.*

*Before the hills in order stood, Or
earth received her frame, From everlasting
Thou art God, To endless years the same.*

*A thousand ages in Thy sight Are
like an evening gone; Short as the watch that
ends the night Before the rising sun.*

*Time, like an ever-rolling stream, Soon
bears us all away; We fly forgotten,
as a dream Dies at the opening day.*

*O God, our Help in ages past, Our
Hope for years to come, Be Thou our Guard while
life shall last. And our eternal Home.*[1]

To me this hymn typifies the faith of my childhood — God as Rock, Refuge, Shelter, Hope and Home. God was rather distant, but His Son was closer and easier to relate to as Friend and Brother.

When I think about some of the parables and the highlights of the Bible that I learned as a child and tried to practice as a youth, I recall the "Golden Rule," "forgive seventy times seven," "love your enemy," the Beatitudes, "turn the other cheek," "the Truth shall set you free," and the Two Great Commandments: "You shall love the Lord your God with your whole heart, with your whole soul, and with all your mind. This is the greatest and first commandment. The second is like it: You shall love your neighbor as yourself. On these two commandments the whole law is based, and the prophets as well.'' (Matthew 22:37-40) (Refer to Appendix II)

So what did Jesus ask of the apostles and what does He ask of me? I have selected ten mandates from Scripture and from my early Catholic training. Jesus asks for Faith in Him, a Free Will decision, Love, Responsibility, commitment to the Truth, acceptance of Suffering and Death, participation in the Resurrection, openness to Healing and Forgiveness, acknowledgement of Mystery and Paradox, and receptivity to Grace. There are certainly other Christian values, but to me, these epitomize Christian belief.

Faith. Faith is a gift from God, and as a gift it must first be accepted. There is an individual call by Jesus and there is an individual response by the disciple. Faith is not a feeling, but an act of the will. It demands discipleship and trust. We see this in the call of the first disciples after their huge catch (''At the sight of this, Simon Peter fell at the knees of Jesus saying, 'Leave me, Lord. I am a sinful man.' For indeed, amazement at the catch they had made seized him and all his shipmates . . . . Jesus said to Simon, 'Do not be afraid. From now on you will be catching men.' With that they brought their boats to land, left everything and became his followers.'' (Luke 5:8-11). No explanations?! No questions?! We see it in the centurion's request of Jesus to cure his servant (''When he was only a short distance from the house, the centurion sent friends to tell him: 'Sir, do not trouble yourself, for I am not worthy to have you enter my house. That is why I did not presume to come to you myself. Just give the order and my servant will be cured . . . . Jesus showed amazement on hearing this, and turned to the crowd which was following him to say, 'I tell you, I have never found so much faith among the Israelites.' '' (Luke 7:6-9). And we find it in Peter in his profession of faith ('' 'And you,' he said to them, 'who do you say that I am?' 'You are the Messiah,' Simon Peter answered, 'the Son of the living God!' Jesus replied, 'Blest are you, . . . No mere man has revealed this to you, but my heavenly Father.' " (Matthew 16:15-17). For his faith, Simon had his name changed by Jesus.

The gift that is faith. Sometimes it may seem like faith is a concept off in the distance somewhere that does not require much action or involvement on my part. But at other times it can be very real. A man was walking by himself on a beautiful summer day just appreciating nature in all its splendor. As he approached the edge of a cliff to survey the panorama of the valley below, a huge gust of wind blew him toward the edge, he lost his balance, and he began to plummet. Screaming and flailing as he fell, his arm snatched a sapling that was trying to eke out an existence on the rocky cliff's face. He managed to grab the small tree with his other arm while simultaneously uttering every prayer he had ever learned. He began yelling, "Help me, God!" After a few minutes, which to him seemed like hours, a deep, solemn Voice from the top of the cliff answered, "Are you sure you want Me to help you?" The man replied with joy and disbelief, "Uh, is that You, God? Yes, I'm sure I want You to help me!" The Voice repeated the same question and the man gave the same reply. Then the Voice said, "Let go." The man said "What?" The Voice said, "Let go." The man said, "Here I am hanging on for dear life, pleading with God to save me, and you're telling me to 'Let go.'?" After a few seconds, the man yelled up to the top of the cliff, "Is there anyone *else* up there?"

Free Will. Free will, freedom, choice, decision — these are all part of our human nature given by God and entrusted to man. There is the image of the call by God and the response by man. But Jesus does not tolerate the "fence straddler." "No servant can serve two masters . . . ." (Luke 17:13), and in another place, "He who is not with me is against me, and he who does not gather with me scatters." (Matthew 12:30) And in the Book of Revelation, a disciple of Jesus comments on Christ's call for decision, "I know your deeds; I know you are neither hot nor cold. How I wish you were one or the other — hot or cold! But because you are lukewarm, neither hot nor cold, I will spew you out of my mouth!" (Revelation

3:15-16) I am not forced to be a Believer, but by my choice to be one, I should not expect a "rose garden." Sometimes detachment from friends or family or relationships is necessary. Although Jesus is the Prince of Peace, He forewarns us of tough times ahead: "Do not suppose that my mission on earth is to spread peace. My mission is to spread, not peace, but division. I have come to set a man at odds with his father, a daughter with her mother, a daughter-in-law with her mother-in-law: in short, to make a man's enemies those of his own household. Whoever loves father or mother, son or daughter, more than me is not worthy of me. He who will not take up his cross and come after me is not worthy of me. He who seeks only himself brings himself to ruin, whereas he who brings himself to naught for me discovers who he is." (Matthew 10:34-39) Whoa! I would say that this comes under the heading of one of those "hard sayings" in the gospels. Furthermore, like accepting the gift of faith, the free will decision to be a disciple is not a one-shot deal, but a daily, life-long process.

Love. "I give you a new commandment: Love one another. Such as my love has been for you, so must your love be for each other. This is how all will know you for my disciples: your love for one another." (John 13:34-35) The followers of Jesus are not known by a certain uniform, by a secret password, by financial status, by power or influence. Rather they are set apart by the company they keep — Jesus and loving as He did. Jesus is an Equal Opportunity Lover. He tells us that our life is simply to be one of love and service: to love God, our neighbor and ourself. We find this in the Two Great Commandments as well as the Ten Commandments. God's love is unconditional and transforming. God loves us just because we *are*, and He wants us to *be* who we *are*. Seems simple enough! But knowing "*how* we are," He gave us a lifetime to work on it.

Not many of us know what unconditional love is and few of us want to be changed when we love someone. But as a Christian I can find myself in places and situations and with people that I would not ordinarily seek out. Jesus asks more than rhetorically, "Who is my neighbor?" and "Who are my brothers?" But the promise is made that by seeing Jesus in our fellow man, we in fact see Jesus, and in turn, by seeing Jesus, we see the Father. The "least of my brethren" show up in the darndest places! Like the beggar with the cup in his hand outside the cathedral who symbolically slaps your Christianity in the face when you walk out of mass; like the pregnant teenager who rides the bus occasionally, looking forelorn and tattered; and like that guy that you work with who really "gets under your skin." Furthermore, we're even supposed to love our enemies! (Let's get real here!) Nevertheless, of the three great virtues, Faith, Hope and Love, Love is the greatest and is everlasting. And since God **Is** Love I can place myself in His transforming care.

Responsibility. Jesus makes it clear that as a Christian I must take responsibility *for* myself and my salvation and that I have a responsibility *to* others as well as to the Father. I am called to be moral, to live the commandments, to love and to serve. I alone am responsible for my spiritual growth and development and my faith commitment. I cannot abdicate it to Father So-and-So or to my spouse or my parents. Jesus did not say "Come, follow Me by remote control" or "Follow Me indirectly." I am charged with striving to have a correctly formed conscience and then follow the dictates of that conscience. Free will gives me the ability to respond with a "yes" or a "no" to the call to discipleship. I imagine that it can be a lonely place, standing before my God.

I also have a responsibility to my neighbors, my brothers and sisters, and to the community, Christian and otherwise. My faith and my love do not exist in a vacuum. Nor am I in a phone booth with God on hold. My responsibility is to make my faith come alive. As G. K. Chesterton said, I should pray as though everything depended on God, and work as though everything depended on me.

Truth. In John's Gospel Jesus says that He is "the way, and the truth, and the life . . . ." (John 14:5) and "If you live according to my teaching, you are truly my disciples; then you will know the truth, and the truth will set you free.'' (John 8:31-32) Commentaries tell us that "truth" refers to fidelity and being set free from sin. Truth also reflects reality, fact and existence. God loves us. Jesus is God's Son who came to save us. We are all children of God. God is in me and you. Jesus is God's Truth. Since I am created in God's image and likeness, then I, too, am a reflection of God's truth if I am faithful.

Suffering And Death; and Resurrection. The Paschal Mystery refers to the life, suffering, death and resurrection of Jesus. As the Pasch or Lamb, He won the victory over death and freed us from sin. He showed us the mystery that resurrection comes from suffering through death. Anyone who has ever planted a seed has experienced the amazement of an apparently inert lifeform that when watered and given light begins to sprout and grow. The transformations are often incredible as the plant grows and blossoms. The fruit then ripens and gives way to withering and then to seed, to start the process over again. This great parable of Jesus is so simple yet so profound and so reflective of our human life.

We are not merely sinful. We are also saved! We all have the potential to transcend our old, earthly, sinful self and to rise to a new, spirit-filled, grace-full self. But the mechanism at first glance seems to be counter-productive: self-denial, acceptance of pain and suffering, losing one's self and losing one's life. But this is the Paschal Mystery to which we are called. This is the roadmap that Jesus left us. As Jesus told Martha after her brother Lazarus died, "I am the resurrection and the life: whoever believes in me, though he should die, will come to life; and whoever is alive and believes in me will never die." (John 11:25-26)

Healing And Forgiveness. Confession, penance, repentance, *metanoia* (a dramatic conversion or change of heart), and the need for forgiveness are traditional concepts that I remember from my youth. Through Christ's resurrection He has conquered sin, brokenness, separation, isolation and division. In Luke Chapter 5, Jesus shows the parallel between forgiveness of sins and curing the paralytic man. It is well known that the Protestant tradition has emphasized the reading of Scripture more than pre-Vatican II Catholic tradition. Healing services were conducted by Oral Roberts or some preacher in a tent. However, the Gospels are full of the miracles and cures that Jesus performed (I counted at least ten in Mark and seven in Matthew). To me, this is one of the major developments in modern Catholicism, the acknowledgement of healing ministries among laity and clergy and religious alike. Forgiveness occurs on emotional, psychological and spiritual levels; healing, on physical, emotional, psychological, and spiritual levels.

It is curious that despite the name change from Confession to Sacrament of Reconciliation, use of this sacrament has been on the decrease, while acceptance of healing ministries has increased. There seems to have been a reaction to the sense of guilt and the need for frequent, weekly confession (which I remember from my childhood), to a more holistic need for healing and reconciliation on more levels than just the spiritual. An example of this is the fact that the original translation of the Catholic mass from Latin to English contained this prayer just prior to receiving Eucharist: "Lord, I am not worthy to receive you, but only say the Word and my *soul* shall be healed." After a number of years it was changed to: "Lord, I am not worthy to receive you, but only say the Word and *I* shall be healed."

Mystery And Paradox. Perhaps one of the more difficult concepts is the element of Mystery and Paradox. Sometimes it's easier to take that "blind leap of faith" and believe that Jesus is the Son of God and that He rose from the dead and conquered sin. Sometime it's more difficult to deal with the things that are more practical and "down to earth," such as losing myself to find myself, losing my life to have life, believing that death leads to life, loving my enemy, being perfect as the Father is perfect, and accepting that Jesus came to divide, and that Jesus came to fulfill the Spirit of the Law but yet not throw out the Letter of the Law. One of my favorite phrases is that "God writes straight with crooked lines." But how does this happen? Why does this happen?

There is the further complication of the *evergreaterness* of God. No matter what trait or quality I can ascribe to God in my human mentality, God is always more than that. For example, God is All Just. He is more just than the Supreme Court or any other judicial body I can think of. Therefore He is More. Besides being All Just, He is also All Merciful. So which trait wins out, God's Justice or God's Mercy? And on and on.

Again, the Gospels are filled with those "hard sayings," yet Jesus says in Matthew (11:28-30) "Come to me, all you who are weary and find life burdensome, and I will refresh you. Take my yoke upon your shoulders and learn from me, for I am gentle and humble of heart. Your souls will find rest, for my yoke is easy and my burden light." This in itself is a mystery, because anyone who has struggled with the Christian message would agree that often times it is anything but "easy" or "light." I remember when I was in the seminary, coming to the conclusion that, unlike most elements of human experience which get easier with practice, Christianity seemed to get more difficult the more I tried to *live* it.

Grace. Finally, the last mandate of Scripture I would like to mention is Grace. I remember Sister Vianney telling the class that we should be in the "state of grace," but this was not a place on the map. Also, as Mary was, we were to strive to be "full of grace." Grace is God's "love channel" or "medium." It is received through prayer and through the sacraments. It allows God to work in my life and allows me to accept His Gift and to give it away. It is God working in and through me, and in and through other people.

Perhaps an example will help to illustrate the point. In an area that was below sea level and prone to flooding, a powerful storm was brewing. The local media announced that people should begin to evacuate. But Tom was a man of God and he began to pray. A few hours later as water began to fill his yard, his neighbor came over and asked Tom to leave with him and his family, but Tom refused. And Tom prayed. Later that day, the police came by and told Tom to evacuate. By now the water was approaching his doorway. But Tom said he'd stay and they should go help the others. And Tom prayed. By the next morning Tom was up on his porch roof when the Red Cross came by with a boat and asked him to come with them. But he said, "No," because he was praying and God was going to help him. A few hours later as the water forced Tom onto the roof of his house, a National Guard helicopter came to take Tom away, but he still refused citing his faith that God would help him. Well, needless to say Tom drowned. When he went up to heaven he was very upset with God for not answering his prayers for help. When he told this to God, God answered, "I did everything I could to help you; I sent your neighbor, the police, the Red Cross and the National Guard, but you wouldn't listen!" Grace allows us to see God's hand in our life and to be His instrument as well.

These ten scriptural values or mandates are among the cornerstones of our Christian beliefs: Faith; Free Will; Love; Responsibility; Truth; Suffering and Death; Resurrection; Forgiveness and Healing; Mystery and Paradox; and Grace. God always was and always will be. In Him we find everlasting life, which is our goal in this life. But somehow, for some of us, these valucs can get distorted, confused and mis-represented in the course of everyday life. Next we will look at this process and some of the ways this happens.

What do you consider to be the core beliefs of your Christian faith?

Do you agree with the author's Ten Mandates? If not, what would you add?

Can you think of examples that demonstrate these beliefs in your daily activities?

How do you try to live out the Ten Commandments and the Beatitudes? (Refer to Appendix II)

Name someone who unconditionally accepts you. How does that feel?

How does it *feel* for you to be a Christian?

CHAPTER II

The Socialization Process — Church, Family, School, Society

A Mighty Fortress Is Our God

A mighty fortress is our God, A Bulwark never failing;
Our helper he amid the flood of mortal ills prevailing;
For still our ancient foe Doth seek to work us woe;
His craft and pow'r are great, And armed with cruel hate,
On earth is not his equal.

Did we in our strength confide,
Our striving would be losing,
Were not the savior on our side,
The man of God's own choosing;
Dost ask who that may be? Christ Jesus, it is he;
Lord Sabbaoth, his name, From age to age the same,
And he must win the battle.[1]

As a human being it is my nature to think in human terms, the realm of my own experience. When I do this about God, I do it in anthropomorphic terms. God is Father. God sits on a throne and has white hair, a long white beard and writes on a score card. God is judgmental, all-seeing, fair and He can get very angry. One image that comes to mind is Michaelangelo's depiction of creation in the Sistine Chapel, in which the finger of God brings life to the world by His mere touch. Think of other images from your childhood and how many of those are still part of your perspective when conceptualizing God, Jesus or the Holy Spirit.

With a legalistic mentality (right/wrong and good/bad) and an emphasis on conforming, authority figures play a major role in a child's life. The Supreme Authority Figure of course is God and His representatives on earth are one's parents, primarily, and secondarily, clergy and religious, teachers, civil authority, etc. This is part of the normal transference process that one develops at an early age as one grows up. Although I knew God (my parents) loved me, I was also afraid of Him (them). I knew that I needed to be good or He (they) would punish me. They even told me so, and Father did too when I went to Church. I also feared being abandoned by Him (them). The authority figures in my life — priests, nuns, my parents (Ma and Popsy), teachers or adults in general — were always telling me to "be good," whatever that was, or I was "going to *get it*," whatever "it" was.

I guess being "good" was being obedient, respectful, hard-working, quiet, attentive, cooperative, conforming, pure and religious. If I was not "good," I was ignored, yelled at, punished, corrected, embarrassed, and sinful. Furthermore, when I was "bad," or "not good," I made both God and my parents angry. *Now* I see that as having a lot of power — being able to "control" God by making Him angry — but *then* it never occurred to me. I learned about the "wrath of God," hell, "fire and brimstone," God as Judge and the Guardian Angel Scorekeeper who was always on my shoulder and somehow even seemed to get involved with Santa Claus around Christmas with this "being good" stuff!

I learned that love was conditional. It was conditioned on what I *did*, not on who I *was*. This leads one to believe that, as Fr. John Powell, S. J. states, one's "value is somehow outside ourselves. We try to assume an appearance that will please others and gain us loving acceptance. We give up on being ourselves and try to become someone else, someone who will be worthy of recognition and love." [2] If I learned this about my parents, teachers and other authority figures, and even friends, and if my human experience is my basis for conceptualizing God, then what do I make of God's love? So this stuff about the love of God meant He could turn it off, too? If I wasn't "good" to the satisfaction of other people, then I was not "good" period.

And what about expectations — those of my parents, my teachers, the parish priests and nuns, the rest of my family, my friends? What about God's expectations of me? ("In a word, you must be made perfect as your heavenly Father is perfect.") (Matthew 5:48) And then, what about my own expectations of myself? It would seem to be fair to say that there is some pressure and tension in this situation.

I seemed to be absorbing more about the punishing, judgmental God than about the loving Father whose child I was. My parents didn't *tell* me they loved me — I had to *assume* that and infer it from what they did, providing food, shelter, clothing, an education, etc. I experienced little affection or talk of love at home, so God the Father to me was rather stern and forboding. I never heard about calling God, "Daddy," as in "Abba," until I was in the seminary, and even then it was difficult.

I know I was taught about how much God loved me to send His Son to die for me. That was a powerful message. But it also seemed to convey some sense of my being responsible for His death. I remember trying to feel as sorry as I possibly could when I went to confession or especially during Holy Week. If there was balance in the presentation of God's abiding, unconditional love and His mercy versus His anger and judgment, I seemed to be missing the former. Why did it seem that God's punishment and justice outweighed His mercy and love? Maybe because that's the way those attributes were presented. Or maybe because that's the way that I was hearing it. Was this a case where it was felt that people are simply too easy on themselves anyway, so the consequence of sin needs to be emphasized? Why was the Last Judgment and fear of God taking precedence over the mercy of Jesus with Mary Magdelene, the woman caught in adultery and the "Good Thief?"

Everyone knows about the well-developed sense of guilt that we Christians, especially those of us of the Catholic variety, possess. When I was growing up, weekly confession was the expectation and there seemed to be an obsession with sinfulness, and the legalistic view about whether something was a mortal sin that killed the soul, or a venial one that merely wounded it. I remember going through a period of scrupulosity for some months when I was in seventh or eighth grade. I would have to talk to Fr. Joe privately for a few minutes before mass to check out whether my list of three or four things were in fact sins, and if so, whether I had to confess them before going to communion. (He was very patient with me.) I was depending on someone else to tell me whether I had sinned or not!

Somehow I was starting to get the message that it was not just what I *did* that was bad, but perhaps that *I* was bad. I had low self-esteem, and felt inferior. My parents felt that way too, possibly because of our nationality (they had experienced some real discrimination against "Dumb Pollocks"), their lack of education and ability to express themselves, the neighborhood we lived in which was right across from the railroad yard, the condition of our house with only a half bath and poor bathing facilities, and being dependent on (renting from) my father's mother for 31 years. I was internalizing these things, along with their frustration and their acceptance of the projections and stereotypes of society.

John Bradshaw and others make the point that *guilt* is feeling bad about something I *did*, and *shame* is feeling bad about who I *am*. With criticism, lack of affection, lack of support, lack of communication, lack of expression of feelings except anger, conditional love and rampant workaholism from my parents; and with an emphasis on discipline, sin as hurting God, control and rigidity, "being good," more negative reinforcement than praise, principles such as "God is first, my Neighbor is second, and I am last" (my wife received this on a holycard as a child) and sort of a religious "boot camp" atmosphere in parochial school, I began feeling bad about myself. I felt shame. I was ashamed. I blushed easily, was embarrassed easily and felt self-conscious. (This was prior to the normal adolescent awkwardness and growth process.) And,

I'm not sure, but perhaps I felt the ultimate shame of not being "good enough" for God to bother saving.

In a workaholic family there is a logical progression. If I am what I do, and what I did was sinful or bad, then I am bad. As Bradshaw and others have said, we become human *doings* rather than human *beings*. Love was conditioned on what I did, how I did it and when I did it. There was criticism for something that was not done, or not done well enough, but little praise for something well done. There was also no rejoicing in just being my parents' son! How, then, could I take solace in just being a Child of God! I had to DO, and I had to try to EARN love. It was not freely given in my experience. And, needless to say, earning God's love is impossible. Although doomed to failure from the outset, this is what I set out to do from an early age.

There seemed to be some guiding principle somewhere in my family, school and church, maybe in my neighborhood or even in our society that went something like this: Children are too proud, vain, boastful, self-centered, and "full of themselves" by nature; therefore praise must be meted out in minute doses on rare occasions. Otherwise you'll have a full-blown, un-Christian egomaniac on your hands! (However, this is the normal narcissistic developmental stage of childhood. In a dysfunctional family the child needs to "be broken" from this as one would a wild pony. But it can also break the child's "spirit.") This may seem far-fetched to some, but very real to others. "We mustn't let Teddy get a big head by praising him and telling him what a good job he's done!" After all, praise must be subdued. This seems akin to the one about "Spare the rod and spoil the child."

"Praise" seemed to be too close to "pride," and, after all, pride was the sin that got Adam and Eve, and therefore us, in all this trouble. Criticism, a checklist mentality, and our sinfulness were reinforced by Confession or the Sacrament of Penance. And then there was that other four letter word ... SELF. It primarily had negative connotations as I remember the word, the exception, perhaps, being, "I did it myself," or "Do it yourself." The word "self" seemed too close to "self-ish" which equals "sinful" which equals "bad." As John Powell, S. J., puts it: "Conditioned as we are by our culture, we seem to be emotionally allergic to the very vocabulary of love of self. The thought of rejoicing in and celebrating our own unique goodness seems like a very distant and alien thought. Immediate associations of egotism, vanity and self-ishness rush like dark clouds into our minds."[3]

The other side of the coin, self-denial, was all too familiar. After all, this was the stuff that saints were made of! Every Lent there was a challenge of how to deprive myself and what to "give up." Not to belittle fasting and penance, but as a matter of balance, it seemed to be out of kilter. "Self" seemed to disappear from this word too, leaving just "DENIAL." "I don't really want that" or "I don't really feel that" or "I don't really care that" led to "I'm not really sure that" or " "I don't really know that." The repetition of doubt and uncertainty resulted in more questions like "How should I feel?" and "What should I think?" Who will tell me? What would a good Christian feel, or do, or say in this time, place or circumstance? Trying to second-guess and emulate others like the saints, or Jesus or Father or Sister was becoming the way to be, as was hoping, that despite throwing a dart in the darkness, I could still hit the target.

I remember my mother telling me "You shouldn't feel that way" or "Don't *be* like that." I also remember being glued to the television that weekend in November 1963 after President Kennedy had been killed and watching live as Jack Ruby shot Lee Harvey Oswald. I yelled, as a boy of fourteen, "Good!" He deserved it. He had killed my hero. In perhaps one of the most tender moments I can recall with my father, he explained that just because Oswald had done something bad was not a reason to be happy about something bad happening to him. It was a very crisp feeling for a kid who blotted out and hid so many of them. However, I confessed it later. I thought it was un-Christian to have the feeling.

I vividly recall an incident when I was about five and a friend of my mother's came over with her young son of about the same age. You have to understand that I didn't get many new toys of my own; most were hand-me-downs from my brothers. But it so happens that I had just gotten a little truck that carried toy logs. It was a really neat truck! Well, when my mother's friend's son saw it, he *had* to play with it. I couldn't share all the old toys, I had to share my new truck, Ma said. I watched his every move as he rough-housed with it, and I hadn't even had it long enough to break it in. He not only broke it in, but he broke it period, along with my heart! My mother never said a word as I grieved quietly over my truck and my feelings. I and they were discounted over the great principle of sharing.

Father Martin Padovani states that if he had a dollar for every time someone confessed a feeling as a sin, he'd be a billionaire![4] Feelings are not sinful; behaviors are. (Remember the three criteria for a mortal sin? It must be a serious matter, I must know that it's wrong, and I must want to do it.) Is a feeling in and of itself a serious or grievous matter? Are my feelings always that cut and dry, or do I spend a lot of time and energy trying to understand them and myself? Do I want to *do* my feelings — for example, turn hate into murder, or greed into theft?

Certainly, this is a complicated issue, but I think it's fair to say that a feeling inherently is not generally sinful. Jesus got angry with the money changers in the Temple, He was frustrated with the disciples who couldn't stay up with Him to pray for an hour in the Garden, and He seemed to lose patience with them in their slowness to catch on to the message He was teaching them. But we're also told that He was like us "in all things but sin." But trying to repress the feelings of anger, envy, jealousy, resentment, disappointment, sorrow, etc., and, believing they are sinful and therefore pretending not to have them — denying their existence — leads to much difficulty. Where did this notion of feelings as being sinful come from? Father John Powell, S. J., says that we *moralize emotions*:

"Depending on our background, we tend to label certain emotions 'good' or 'bad.' "[5] This leads to *"should*'s," *"ought*'s," and *"don't*'s." We were brought up with sayings like "Children should be seen and not heard," and "If you don't have something nice to say, don't say it at all." So you stuff the feelings after a while, especially if you think that just having them is a sin. This then becomes the rules of the dysfunctional family: don't talk, don't trust, don't feel.[6] Don't talk, especially about your feelings. Don't have the feelings to begin with, especially if they're not "good," positive feelings. And don't trust yourself or your own feelings period. You need to check out what other people are feeling or saying to see if you're safe.

We weren't supposed to talk in Church, we weren't supposed to talk in class, and talking was not encouraged at home. Silence seemed to work out better, because it didn't stir up any trouble or disagreements. The image I have is that of sitting on the lid of a pressure cooker, or tiptoeing around the "sleeping giant" of emotion so as not to wake it. Self-expression, not just verbal, seemed to be discouraged. Is it any wonder that I found myself a shy, introverted teenager who was able to answer questions but who couldn't "make small talk"? People would always comment on how quiet I was. Even today in social situations I seem to run out of things to say.

The other end of that two-way process was also a problem — finding someone who would listen. In my family, there are a lot of interruptions of one's train of thought and we're a bunch of loud talkers, because the louder you speak, the better your chances are of being heard and of getting your point across. Conversation seems to have focused on facts or events rather than on one's feeling state. And with my mother's chronic illness and various health problems that my siblings and I have, "How are you feeling?" more often than not referred to one's physical health rather than one's emotional health. This was brought home to me a few years ago when my sister commented that she didn't really *know* me because I was so wishy-washy in the sense of not making *my* feelings known and always wanting to pacify and say how well things were going even if they weren't going well. I had confessors in the seminary who certainly listened as did my few close friends, but many other people seemed to merely bounce off what I said to them. I felt discounted and ignored.

I remember thinking of emotions as something that "got in the way" of my being a good Christian. When I got angry or upset or wanted something for myself or felt that I had done something worth noting, these feelings seemed to go against what I was being taught. I was stuck with these emotions and had to control them for the sake of my salvation. If I was not successful at removing these feelings, then I was sinful and put myself down in addition to the guilt that I felt. Even to think about these feelings was un-Christian, and they were to be banished, as were those impure thoughts. Besides, people's feelings were always "getting hurt," like they were something apart from the whole person. So dissociating from those harmful, painful feelings seemed like a worthwhile endeavor. Plus, I had that nasty stubborn streak common to a Taurus.

Another situation that I remember from my childhood was that when someone "spoke their mind" or expressed their feelings, it usually meant raised voices, expressing anger and "blowing up." You had to be prepared to take the consequences, which among the adults could mean not speaking to each other for weeks, or months or perhaps longer. A few hard, pushy people like my one grandmother could get away with it, but many others had to swallow their feelings in order to avoid the repercussions.

In addition to not talking and not feeling, not trusting entered the picture as well. I don't really remember not trusting my parents or my teachers, but I do remember not trusting myself. This was the case especially in regard to my feelings. I came to not know or recognize or express how I felt, but I got better at guessing or predicting how someone else was going to feel.

This uncertainty affected how I've lived. It occurred to me that, even today, one of the phrases I use when talking about someone or some situation is, "I *guess* that" so-and-so said this or such-and-such happened. Even though I knew something as clear as I knew my own name, after some time would pass, I began to question if I had the story straight. I did not want to say the wrong thing or give the wrong intepretation. This also made me very reluctant to talk about people, for fear of gossiping or slandering someone and committing a sin. Therefore it was easier just to be quiet, even if I might have had a legitimate complaint or criticism. But I could guess what the other person was thinking or feeling. And although I have worked hard, both personally and professionally, at becoming a good listener, my wife especially will point out how I seem to take up the other person's part when listening to her explain a situation or problem. It just seems to be ingrained from so much practice.

This self-doubt also affected my self-confidence, my self-reliance, and my reality-testing ability. I learned to second-guess myself and to doubt if I had the correct perception of a particular situation or incident, especially one involving other people and their feelings. But I was definitely there, waiting in the wings, to take the blame if something went wrong. I learned to ask immediately if something was my fault when something went wrong. I was very subjective rather than objective. If someone was wrong, it was probably me. If something went wrong, it was probably my fault.

There were areas where I did learn not to hope for something, or not to have very high expectations, such as wishing for a gift that I wanted for Christmas or taking a small vacation; I knew we couldn't afford it. I also learned to temper my dreams so they wouldn't get too high into the stars and be totally unachievable. I kept pretty close to the ground so as not to be disappointed.

There is another arena that caused problems of trust, due to mixed messages and double standards. One had to do with the media. To be taught that one is supposed to tell the truth and that "your word is your bond" and then come up against things like "Don't believe everything you read" caused problems for me. To understand that people will say things or write things just to be sensational or sell newspapers, was not easy. To read about politicians or other public figures saying one thing on one day and another thing on the next day caused confusion. For example, there were statements in the Nixon Era when something was said one day and the next day it was "inoperative." In other words, a lie. Or in 1960 when our U-2 spy plane was shot down, it took a while for President Eisenhower to admit that we even had such a plane. The United States didn't spy on other countries. Only the Russians did! These things made me wonder: does giving one's word or making a statement mean anything? Are all people to be stereotyped as are politicians or used car salesmen? How does one resolve the contradictions? What about the times when the fuzzy line that separates Church and State in our country was crossed?

Even now, the issue is a concern. What, for instance, about the role played by religion? You see these people going to church, etc., yet it doesn't seem to make a difference in their lives — they almost run you over in the parking lot after church! Or, how about the organized crime families who seemed to be so "religious" on the outside, yet so ruthless on the inside? Or what about all the wars that have been fought in the name of religion or seemingly under God's protection? What about situations in the Church, such as that portrayed in the book *Joshua*, where truly Christ-like behavior to bring about unity of different faiths is met with suspicion, mistrust and hate? In the same book, there is division in the name of religion rather than true spirituality in the name of religion. What about Church law, such as that about not eating meat on Fridays, which was subsequently changed? What about religion being an addiction, a point raised by Father Leo Booth? In fact, much of the Gospel message is a "double edged sword" and contains seeming contradictions such as: "judge not, lest you be judged"; by giving, we receive; the first shall be last, and the last shall be first; by dying to self, we are born to life; by forgiving, we are forgiven; and "turn the other cheek." Yet we see Jesus' anger at the money changers, and Jesus saying that He came to cause division even in one's own family! These concepts would be difficult to comprehend under "normal" circumstances, and are even more troublesome because of the process that we have been describing.

If we believe and trust that a Christian's goal in life is to return to the Father in heaven, why is there so much grief and distress at funerals? It was not too long ago that the Church changed the color of a funeral Mass from sorrowful black to joyous white. If our faith is so strong and we believe with such vigor, why do we worry so much and become so distraught? I could never understand that about my mother. As much as she prayed and believed in God, that still could not remove the pain of chronic worry from her life. She could not turn that over to God completely. She had to hold on. My brothers and sister and I would say that she "was not happy unless she was worrying about someone." But what a burden to bear. Now, in her later years, I see how much it pains her that she has no control over this compulsion.

There are two societal stereotypes that played a major role in our socialization process concerning gender-specific behavior. They, too, give mixed signals between the Christian ideal and the societal norm. One had to do with girls learning the maternal instincts of a caretaker, being a "good" mother and pleasing the family — making them happy. Girls were "made of sugar and spice and everything nice." Boys, on the other hand, were supposed to be rough and tough and not cry. They were not supposed to show emotion unless it was aggressive or defensive. Also, except in certain ethnic groups, boys were not encouraged to show affection. I'm sure most of us remember, and some of us have said, those famous words, "You're going to cry . . ., I'll give you something to cry about."

Another paradox is that we as a society are so imbued with the Christian Protestant work ethic that workaholism has been acceptable for generations to the detriment of countless millions of families. That, in turn, is so enmeshed with the "American Dream," that success at any cost has become acceptable as well. Rev. Joseph Gallagher in his book *The Christian Under Pressure* states that psychiatrist Karen Horney "thought that many Americans suffer special conflicts because they belong to a culture which simultaneously idealizes the man who cares about his brother and the man who climbs the rungs of success, even over other people's bodies."[7] We Americans seem to favor the underdog, but we also love our champions. Who remembers who finished second or third in the professional baseball or football playoffs? We are a very competitive society, not only in athletics, but in business, in science and technology, in schools and clubs, and in families. We have thrived for over twenty-five years now on the "thrill of victory and the agony of defeat!" a la "Wide World of Sports." A popular best seller some years ago was titled, *Looking Out for Number One.*

Is there congruence between what we say and what we do? We say that we don't really believe that if someone has financial success and material wealth that it is a blessing from God. We also say that we don't really believe physical suffering and other problems are a sign of God's disfavor with someone. But do we really act that way? Is that the case with other people as well, especially authority figures? I'm sure you're familar with the saying, "Do as I say, not as I do." That one bothered me about my father, so I tried to uphold the same principles for myself as I did for my stepdaughters.

There were a few other mixed messages at home, as well. One was that it was okay to be angry and upset with other family members, but it was not okay to get angry and upset, even if it was a legitimate complaint, with someone outside the family. Seemingly this would reveal something bad or un-Christian about our family to the outside world. Also, my parents prayed a lot and went to Church and the sacraments frequently, but it did not seem to bring a sense of peace, love and intimacy to our home. Perhaps that was our family secret. What happened to Christian love and "charity begins at home?" So why bother? I know that they were not capable of giving something that they were not taught and therefore that they did not *have* to give. But in that regard, their faith did not seem to have an impact on our emotional beings, as children. This is how I saw it, at least. Since my oldest brother is fifteen years older than I, the five of us siblings did not live together at home for very long because Joe went away to school when I was three and Len got married and left home the next year. We do have different memories and perspectives on our childhoods and our growing up years.

Our friend Webster would agree that "trust" and "faith" are synonymous. What are the ramifications of the "don't trust" rule in some families? Could it mean "don't believe," or "don't have faith?" Why bother? You'll only be let down, frustrated, rejected and, eventually, abandoned. Look at what's happened at home or in school or in other relationships. Is that what it's like with God, too? And what if there is no God, no afterlife!? Could it be an unreachable goal, another one of those "doomed to failure" situations, a cruel hoax? How do you love Hitler, or Idi Amin, or Saddam Hussein as a Christian? If man is created in God's image, how can there be so many evil ones? One's religion and spiritual upbringing set faith and belief as standards, but if my human experience, the realm in which I live my life, has taught me to be leary of believing and trusting, there is a monumental dilemma set up. In my own life, feeling that my faith was inadequate to be in a leadership role in the Church was one of my reasons for not continuing into the priesthood.

Clearly, viewing spiritual concepts from the realm of human experience can cause problems when I profess faith, belief and trust in God, the Supreme Authority Figure. Many of the above conflicts are well hidden and become apparent only after much reflection on one's experience. These conflicts can, however, begin to explain the difficulties that some of us have had with our faith, our God, ourselves and our relationships.

Although faith is not a feeling, when I felt isolated and separated from God, I sensed that both faith and God's love were conditioned upon my response. If this was to be strictly an intellectual affair and my feelings were the culprit, then I was prepared to learn to keep them harnessed and in check as best I could. After all, wasn't "getting emotional" a negative state to be in? Wasn't it a sign of losing control? God forbid that I should be out of control!

For centuries the Catholic Church was an emotional desert. It was stoic, pompous, formal, reverent, orderly, controlled, and without feeling. That was the way it was supposed to be. Today, I can hardly believe that as I was growing up wanting to be a priest, the Mass was still in Latin! We "baby boomers" and those older than us look back and see the isolation that was present in the Church's liturgy with the Mass in a "dead," foreign language, no talking in the Church building, no communication with the other attendees, and a kind of "talk-to-God-from-my-phonebooth" mentality, with each person in their own isolation chamber, reading a prayer book or saying the rosary etc. Is it any wonder that some people had a difficult time with such things as the Kiss of Peace in which you were actually supposed to touch someone and talk to them? There were centuries of religious and emotional cobwebs that needed to be dusted away. It was now acceptable to relate to others at Mass! There could also be lively music and even some clapping and expressions of emotion like smiling or hugging. We could now borrow from some of our Protestant brethren and *feel* at liturgy or other communal activities.

One of the main virtues that impressed me as I was growing up was humility. Jesus spoke about it at the Sermon on the Mount ("How blest are the poor in spirit: the reign of God is theirs . . . . Blest are the lowly; they shall inherit the land." (Matthew 5:3, 5) And again when He said, "The greatest among you will be the one who serves the rest. Whoever exalts himself shall be humbled, but whoever humbles himself shall be exalted." (Matthew 23:11-12) In another place, He said "Many who are first shall come last, and the last shall come first." (Matthew 19:30) The word "humble" is defined as "lowly," "without pride" and "meek." Synonyms as a verb include "degrade" and "humiliate," and as an adjective, "submissive," "common," and "poor." I learned all varieties of this word, and it was with the expectation of being a good Christian. I learned it especially from the good nuns and from my parents. It was good to go unnoticed, to blend into the woodwork, to be unassuming, to give in, to be quiet, to be obedient, to conform, to be passive, to be ordinary, to serve, to defer to others, to take care of others and to please other people. Sameness (not "making waves" or attracting attention) and fitting the mould or the stereotype were "good."

Being different or being a non-conformist was "bad." Conformity was pitted against individuality, and passivity versus assertiveness. We children were always told to "give *good* example." It was holy and desirable to be as meek and lowly as possible. Imitation of the Suffering Lamb of God was admirable as was bearing one's crosses joyfully. This made it easier to take abuse (not physical or sexual, but in the sense of being used or taken advantage of) from others and it became seemingly normal to heap abuse upon myself. The more abuse one took, the better one's Christian life. It seemed to be logical! All done in the name of the Lord . . . .

Another related issue was the second great commandment: "You shall love your neighbor as yourself." (Matthew 22:39) In light of the above discussion, somehow in that commandment, I heard "Love your neighbor *instead* of yourself, love your neighbor *more than* yourself, love your neighbor *in spite of* yourself." I heard that my neighbor and I were on a teeter-totter and my job was always to try to be on the ground, on the bottom; and to keep my neighbor up above me, high in the air. When I did this I was doing what I was supposed to do. This was being a good Christian.

Jesus did say, "love your neighbor as yourself." Now, I see that that statement implies the equality of the two components, "neighbor" and "yourself." But for most of my life I did not see it as equality, but rather as subserviance of self to neighbor. Again, I'm not sure where that came from. I don't know whether I was really taught that or whether I was taught equality at all, but all these mixed messages and subtle signs changed my perspective. Regardless of the source, however, I do know that I lived with that perception for a long time. After thinking that way and feeling that way, I began to believe that way. Therefore, other people *were* better than I was. When I compared myself with peers or others that I admired, by choosing their strong points, I inevitably seemed to come up short. This in turn reinforced my low self-esteem, but also seemed to be in the Christian scheme of things. This was a "hard pill to swallow" and contributed to a lot of the depression I felt as a teenager.

Finally, I would like to look at a behavioral principle that I was taught by the director of a private counseling practice that I became affiliated with some years ago. That principle is this: feelings follow behavior, not the other way around. In other words, if I keep doing what I have always done, I will continue to feel the way I have always felt. I cannot simply hope and pray and wait for my feelings to change. It will never happen unless my behavior, my actions, change first.

What this means, in this discussion of the socialization process, is that as I continued to act as someone who was inferior, uncertain, hesitant, guilty, shameful, martyred, empty, overworked, persecuted, scattered, self-doubting, humble, uncommunicative, perfectionistic, depressed and sinful, I could not help but *feel* that way, even if I couldn't recognize or put a label on the feelings. And the vicious cycle was that these actions seemed to be the norm, the goal, the Christian thing to do. These actions were reinforced by the messages from home, school, church and society. Therefore, the feelings were often negative and therefore "frozen" or stuffed. As Ernie Larsen says about co-dependent behavior, "What we live with, we learn; what we learn, we practice; what we practice, we become; and what we become has conseqences."[8] Boy, does it have consequences!

As long as I acted with the above list as my roadmap, I could not feel adequate, certain, self-assured, validated, shameless, full of life, resourceful, relaxed, calm, peaceful, confident, proud, friendly, competent, happy and saved! Something had to give, but I wasn't sure what. It seemed like I couldn't win for losing.

Now that we have seen some of the factors and influences contributing to this child's, this teenager's, this young adult's struggle to be a "good Christian" while living as an other-dependent person, let's picture what this non-recovering co-dependent Christian looks like.

Reflection/Discussion Questions

What are some of your images of God? From the past? Today?

What are some of the "mixed messages" you received as you were growing up? From whom did you get these messages? How did the messages affect you? Are they still affecting you?

Who taught you, or how did you learn these messages? Have you taught these messages to your children, friends, co-workers?

Did you experience conditional love? How did that affect you?

How does society promulgate double standards/conditional love/mixed messages? How does your Church do this?

Did you experience the "don't talk, don't feel, don't trust" rules?

Would you say that your parents, teachers, clergy were/are co-dependent?

Do you consider yourself to be a humble person? How do you understand humility?

Have you tried to change your feelings by wishing, hoping, praying, acting? What has worked best for you?

What physical symptoms do you have that reflect emotional origin, whether positive or negative?

In what ways does your family, society, Church support/degrade you?

Recall a childhood experience that changed you/your life in some way.

What tends to immobilize you?

Think about whether you have ever experienced inner panic about getting what you had hoped for and then sabotaging it? Why did this happen?

CHAPTER III

The Non-Recovering Co-Dependent Christian And The Ten Mandates

Prayer Of St. Francis

Make me a channel of your peace.
Where there is hatred, let me bring your love.
Where there is injury, your pardon, Lord.
And where there's doubt, true faith in you.

Make me a channel of your peace.
Where there's despair in life, let me bring hope.
Where there is darkness — only light,
And where there's sadness ever joy.

Oh, Master, grant that I may never seek
So much to be consoled as to console,
To be understood as to understand,
To be loved, as to love, with all my soul.

Make me a channel of your peace.
It is in pardoning that we are pardoned,
In giving of ourselves that we receive,
And in dying that we're born to eternal life.[1]

The words to this prayer/song are difficult for the co-dependent Christian, especially one who is not in a recovery program. The difficulty stems from the fact that the words represent such an ideal and they seem so self-emptying for a person who already feels empty. The Christian ideal is evident, but the individual, who is trying so hard to fulfill it, is screaming, "*I* need to be consoled, *I* need to be understood, *I* need to be loved, TOO!" "I can't give it, if I don't have it!"

The prayer is so other-centered that it's precisely the kind of message the non-recovering, co-dependent Christian needs to hear in order to keep the vicious cycle going. I remember feeling that "You can't get blood out of a turnip," and "I'm so drained that there's nothing left to give." In the socialization process described previously, we have learned our lessons well. In repeating the same behaviors time after time, the feelings of low self-esteem, inadequacy, perfectionism, controlling, fear, anxiety, shame and unworthiness continue to follow as day follows night.

The sense of having an indentity seems to be confused and eventually lost by being so wrapped up in this other-centeredness, which is sanctioned by the Judaeo-Christian tradition. The dilemma calls up the story about the man who was walking in a remote, barren, desert-like area of a country with his friend. Next to them walked a beast of burden, an ass. They came upon a traveller going in the opposite direction.

They paused to talk a while, and the traveller made the comment that the ass was a beast of burden and surely one of them should ride the ass instead of both of them walking. So one of the two men rode the ass for the next few miles until they came upon a merchant going in the other direction. After talking for a while, the merchant made the comment that it was so hot that both of the men should ride the ass and save their strength. So the two men mounted the animal and proceeded on their journey.

After a time, they came upon a trader loaded down with goods who saw the two riding on the poor animal. He said that the ass would surely die if they continued to ride him, especially under these conditions. He suggested to the two men that they should carry the ass to save its strength. So they bound its feet and got a sturdy pole and carried the animal.

As nightfall approached the sky clouded over and it began to rain heavily. When they came upon a small stream, it began to flood. As they crossed the rickety bridge, it gave way and all three of them fell into the water. The two men swam to safety. But the poor ass, with is feet bound, drowned.

The moral of the story: "If you try to please everybody, you'll lose your ass!" Helping others has its place, but not at the expense of hurting one's self and diverting one from doing God's will. Pleasing others can make one feel good, accepted, even loved, but that is short-lived. In the long run, it can be fatal. I don't view this in the same sense as when Jesus said, ''Whoever would save his life will lose it, but whoever loses his life *for my sake* will find it.'' (Matthew 16:24) (italics added) And often times, where are those people who were pleased? Long gone, down the trail. The non-recovering, co-dependent Christian has a poor sense of self to start. Jesus does not want our worst, He wants our best.

Let's look at this dysfunctional Christian in the context of our ten mandates of Scripture: Faith; Truth; Love; Free Will; Responsibility; Healing and Forgiveness; Suffering and Death; Resurrection; Grace; and Mystery and Paradox. We saw how the socialization process skewed the original ten mandates. Now, let's see how these ten mandates might be affected as the non-recovering, co-dependent Christian tries to put them into practice. (Each mandate will alternately use ''he'' then ''she'' when referring to this individual.)

Faith. How does this individual live out his faith commitment? He sees it as a tug of war, a contest, a struggle — a struggle or tug of war between himself and God. Somehow, in his efforts at controlling and manipulating other people, he knows what is best for them more than God knows what is best for them. He is affected by fear of God and fear of punishment. He is torn away from himself, torn away from other people and torn away from his God. He fears abandonment by God, by parents, by friends and those whom he loves. His faith is conditional, he believes: If he doubts God or his beliefs, then God abandons him. He hopes and prays that God will be his salvation, but the more he believes, the more he seems to be caught in a quagmire: the deeper he gets into relationships with other people, his own feelings, or lack of feelings, send him into depression or despair over these relationships and feelings. These relationships are full of the learned behaviors that we saw in the socialization process.

The "don't talk," "don't trust," "don't feel," "don't believe" rules begin to apply to his relationship with God, too. He has another reason to put himself down — not actually believing what he says he believes. He says he'll "put it in God's hands," but he'll agonize about it, worry, second-guess, etc. Maybe God won't be there!

In a kind of stream of consciousness, he questions: "How can this happen? How can this be? What does my God want of me? Should it be painful to believe? Is it supposed to hurt?"

What does he do with the doubts that he has? Does he express them? Does he live them out? Does he brush them aside? Does he try to deal with them? They say that seeing is believing, but he cannot see — he cannot see his God who is supposed to be in other people. How can he live with this self-doubt? If he has been saved, why does he keep feeling this way? Where is his freedom?

Does growing in faith mean becoming more other-centered? Other people have spoken for him regarding faith for most of his life — at Baptism (infant), at First Eucharist, and even at Confirmation (in the form of parental pressure) which is supposed to be a rite of passage. However, about the only other "adult" thing that occurs around that age (13 to 16) is being charged more to see a movie or getting a driver's license. When does he have a voice?

"I want to do your Will, Lord. But why, why does it hurt so much? Why is it so hard? What's wrong with me? Why do I keep getting into this same situation about doubts and relationships? It seems like it's one thing after another. Or is it the same thing over and over? When will it finally be done, finished?" He needs help and direction, Lord. He knows that he's supposed to let go, but it's so difficult. He knows that it's supposed to be "**Thy** will be done," but it's difficult. Many times, many, many times, its "**My** will be done." He hasn't quite gotten it together yet, believing that the Lord is God, but he lives as if he were God. But his sense of being God is trying to control and direct and manipulate, whereas the Lord's truly being God is based on love and free will in His creation.

"If only I were smarter, if only I had done things differently, if only I were more giving, if only my family were different, if only I were more Christian, then it would be okay. If only . . ., if only." He feels and is aware of his guilt about the past; he worries and is anxious and fearful about his future; and he is frozen, trapped and feels inadequate to move in his present. Faith? "My God, my God why have you forsaken me?"

Truth. In the person of Jesus Christ, we Christians find Truth. As we saw earlier, Truth refers to our salvation and being faithful. But as humans we must concretize this abstract concept and make it a part of our everyday experience. How does a person bring truth to her life? Those of us with relationship problems begin at an early age to make assumptions and presumptions. It seems as though goodness, happiness and salvation are found in the *other* person. But the *Other* is only one part of the mosaic.

As Melody Beattie states, "Needing people too much can cause problems. Other people become the key to our happiness . . . . (Much) of the other-centeredness, orbiting our lives around other people, goes hand in hand with codependency and springs out of our emotional insecurity . . . . (Much) of this incessant approval seeking we indulge in also comes from insecurity. The magic is in others, not us, we believe. The good feelings are in them, not us. The less good stuff we find in ourselves, the more we seek it in others. *They* have it all; we have nothing. *Our* existence is not important. We have been abandoned and neglected so often that we also abandon ourselves."[2]

One truth about our faith is that it is relational and involves other people. Another is that I, too, am a child of God, formed in His image and likeness. But as we saw in the discussion of faith, the co-dependent, non-recovering Christian is also of the mind set to pick and choose what is truth for her. She will accept, for example, the truth that Jesus redeemed her and that Jesus today is seen in the "least of the brethren." But she has great difficulty accepting that she is personally lovable or that she is forgiven. She can accept these teachings in her head but not in her heart. Selectively accepting certain truths and implicitly rejecting others amounts to manipulation of both the Truth and God. Truth becomes distorted, dissected, a lie. The Truth is supposed to "set us free," but the Distorted Truth makes us a captive of our own heart and mind.

Although she may be supported by friends and respected by acquaintances who think highly of her, she has so taken on the perspective of "the other," that she does not feel good about herself and finds it hard to understand what others see in her.

Furthermore, she tries so hard to do the "right thing." Being task-oriented, she is aware of the "carrot at the end of the stick," salvation. Partly out of fear, partly out of compulsion, and partly out of her Christian faith, she "goes for the gold" in the realm of faith, salvation. She gives until it hurts, she tries to "be nice" to other people, she focuses on self-denial. But she does it *her* way and on *her* terms. Besides denying many positive messages about herself, she has to deny things about others as well, such as, their free will, their responsibility, and their openness to God's grace. She is embarrassed to receive gifts and recognition, but will lavish them on others. She has also internalized the messages that "nice guys finish last" and that "the truth hurts." For our "lost Christian," the non-recovering, co-dependent Christian, it really does.

The mixed messages and the resulting confusion from the socialization process present Truth as something that is not clear. In fact, it is rather muddled. There is a conflict between what I know intellectually about my religion and my faith, and what I am feeling about myself and my relationships. Trying to make sense out of this dichotomy can cause an unhealthy emphasis on either one aspect or the other; that is, either becoming a religious fanatic, or abandoning God as a useless complication of my life. Either way, the Christian mandate is lost.

Love. It is supremely Christian. It is the message of the Two Great Commandments. It is what we all need and want.

It is what God gave us first. But it is also what the "lost Christian" misunderstands, misinterprets, and misuses. This is at the core of our problem. The "lost Christian" wants to be liked by everyone. Like the Parable of the Good Shepherd in which the shepherd leaves the ninety-nine sheep to go after the one who is lost, the "lost Christian" discounts the good relationships that he might have and agonizes over the one person he cannot convince to like him. In his extremism he has to like everyone, and everyone must like him. He gets hung up on the directive to "love your enemy."

As with Truth, the meaning of love is confused. According to Scott Peck, author of *The Road Less Travelled*, love is "the will to extend one's self for the purpose of nurturing one's own or another's spiritual growth."[3] According to St. Paul, "Love is patient; love is kind. Love is not jealous, it does not put on airs, it is not snobbish. Love is never rude, it is not self-seeking, it is not prone to anger; neither does it brood over injuries. Love does not rejoice in what is wrong but rejoices with the truth. There is no limit to love's forbearance, to its trust, its hope, its power to endure . . . . There are in the end three things that last: faith, hope and love, and the greatest of these is love." (1 Corinthians 13:4-7, 13) Love is mistaken for needing, rescuing, caretaking, controlling, pitying, sympathizing, enabling, "do-gooding," protecting, admiring, helping, etc. You get the picture. This "lost Christian" wants it so badly that he'll call just about anything "love" in order to fulfill the Biblical order and to try to feel better. And remember, this co-dependent Christian doesn't trust his own feelings so he relies on the other person to decide whether this is love or not. Thus, he gets sucked into unhealthy relationships; rather than being mutually fulfilling and growth-filled, they are self-serving, one-sided and enmeshed, lacking boundaries and identity. And we're also told that love is laying down one's life — to die — for another, so when it hurts to be in a relationship, it may seem to be the Christian thing to do!

Melody Beattie talks about caretaking as fostering anger. She says that both the caretakers and those being taken care of become angry victims of the same dynamics. I see it as going something like this — Helper: "I love you. I tried so hard to help you, and that's the thanks I get! Look at all I've done for you! Well, I'm finished! Enough's enough!" Helpee: "You're smothering me! I can't take it anymore! Leave me alone, PLEASE!" No one wins.

Melody Beattie states: "I think caretaking perverts Biblical messages about giving, loving, and helping. Nowhere in the Bible are we instructed to do something for someone, then scratch his or her eyes out. Nowhere are we told to walk the extra mile with someone, and then grab the person's cane and beat him or her with it. Caring about people and giving are good, desirable qualities — something we need to do — but many co-dependents have misinterpreted the suggestions to 'give until it hurts.' We continue giving long after it hurts, usually until we are doubled over in pain."[4] An example might be a situation in which someone bends over backwards to help someone, to care for them, for months, maybe years, at the same time letting any negative feelings or complaints go unspoken. Meanwhile all this anger is building up inside the helper and when it does come out, it overpowers the helpee and the two may never speak again, or the relationship is changed forever due to "hard feelings."

(As an aside, there is certainly a legitimate place for authority, control, discipline, and caretaking such as relationships between parent and child; judicial and police roles; teachers and childcare workers and the students and children they deal with; nurses and other medical personnel and their patients; legal guardians watching over those who are mentally incompetent; family members and custodial care workers who provide for the physically and mentally challenged, etc. Here, we are speaking of caretaking and controlling, not as healthy, positive traits born of a healthy maturity, but as out of balance, negative characteristics of a co-dependent who feels weak and fearful. However, these co-dependent behaviors can and do occur in the relationships indicated above, especially between parent and child, regardless of age.)

Another misconception is that somehow the co-dependent can, in fact, be "all things to all men." Of course, in his head he knows that only Jesus could wear those shoes, but he can try, can't he? Father Joseph Gallagher cites a former student of his who said ". . . most people are on a journey from what they are not to what they cannot be."[5] To me, this has to do with expectations, those we have of ourselves and those we have of others. This is part of the strings that are attached to the caretaking, the rescuing, the controlling, etc. that we do. The task is impossible, but we are the Don Quixote's of the spiritual realm, ready to rescue at the drop of a kerchief.

Finally, I would like to cite an example of the anger that the "lost Christian" can feel if the payoff is not there, as he expected, for all his "love":

"Meanwhile the elder son was out on the land. As he neared the house on his way home, he heard the sound of music and dancing. He called one of the servants and asked him the reason for the dancing and the music. The servant answered, 'Your brother is home, and your father has killed the fatted calf because he has him back in good health.' The son grew angry at this and would not go in; but his father came out and began to plead with him.

"He said to his father in reply: 'For years now I have slaved for you. I never disobeyed one of your orders, yet you never gave me so much as a kid goat to celebrate with my friends. Then, when *this son of yours* (italics added) returns after having gone through your property with loose women, you kill the fatted calf for him.'

" 'My son,' replied the father, 'you are with me always, and everything I have is yours. But we had to celebrate and rejoice! *This brother of yours* (italics added) was dead, and has come back to life. He was lost, and is found.' " (Luke 15:25-31) Obviously the other son had an hidden agenda as the "lost Christian" usually does. It seems to be love with a catch, what's in it for me? Greater self-esteem, being liked, eternal salvation? (This is the classic compulsive, non-redeemed assistant — No. 2 — in the Enneagram model.)

Free Will. Karl Marx said that religion was the "opiate of the masses." Because of religion they would be passive and docile and accept intolerable conditions as the Will of God. Consequently they would not rise up and revolt and defend themselves.

But we do have free will, a choice. Our "lost Christian," however, feels that she does not have a *real* choice. Basically there are only two options in the co-dependent's view, self and other. And most of the time, she chooses the other at the expense of herself. After years of this, it becomes second nature and any choice gradually fades away. As with all addictions, compulsion replaces freedom to choose and she feels trapped. She is programmed and has no alternative other than to act as a people-pleasing, controlling caretaker who tries to tell herself that she is doing God's will but feels like hell while doing it! In that sense, religion does become an opiate, a drug, which keeps her from standing up for her own rights. She does the behaviors that she has learned so well and she feels the way she has gotten used to feeling. When she does think "I can't take this anymore! I've got to do something!" her religious beliefs step in and invalidate those feelings and help keep her a prisoner inside herself. The voice of God that she believes she hears inside herself tells her that she should "offer it up" and that she's "being good" by helping others and caring for them. She remembers that God is in other people but forgets that He's in her as well.

Her ability to choose is impaired in other ways, too. She has difficulty making decisions without cheking out other people and their feelings and desires first. Because of her uncertainty, she, more often than not, chooses to go with the flow rather than breaking out of the mould. And while this is not uncommon in human nature as a whole, it is particularly troublesome here because of the apparent sanction of the behavior by religion and the resulting negative consequences on the victim, the "lost Christian." What was once a decision to be a Christian, if embraced or else re-affirmed when one is an adult, has boomeranged into a self-deprecating strangle hold that is choking the very life out of this individual.

Responsibility. Another of our Christian mandates is responsibility. We are "response-able." Being called by Jesus to be His disciples, we accept the challenge. In Genesis, after Cain killed Abel, we are told, "Then the Lord asked Cain, 'Where is your brother Abel?' He answered, 'I do not know. Am I my brother's keeper?' " (Genesis 4:9) The inference, of course, is "Yes." In Luke's Gospel after hearing that we are to love our neighbor as ourself, a lawyer (how appropriate) asks Jesus to clarify: "And who is my neighbor?" The response is that the Good Samaritan was the man's neighbor.

Jesus says, "Then go and do the same." (Luke 10:29, 37) With these messages from his religion, and having learned co-dependent behavior at home, at school and in relationships, the "lost Christian" has ample evidence to "do the same." He slowly learns that he is responsible for almost everyone and everything. He has very few boundaries and doesn't know when to say "No." He is conscientious, dependable, reliable, a joiner and volunteer, often a workaholic, perfectionistic, and hard on himself and others as well. He is preoccupied with serving others and he does not take adequate care of himself. To die a martyr or in the line of Christian duty is his, perhaps un-conscious, goal. He spreads himself too thin, gets burned out, and is used and abused. He's the guy who does a fantastic job at work and the boss can always count on him.

And what is his reward? A raise? A few perks? No, . . . more work! Like the old Tennessee Ernie Ford song, for shoveling his sixteen tons of coal each day, he gets "another day older and deeper in debt." (A recent tour of a Pennsylvania coal mine indicated that sixteen tons of coal was a typical miner's daily quota — four carloads of four tons each.) This Hero tends to be employed in the helping professions, such as, so-cial worker, counselor, nurse, clergyperson, minister, teacher, etc. because these roles provide sanctioned avenues for his com-pulsion. (The Hero is one of four basic roles played by children in a dysfunctional family. The others are Scapegoat, Lost Child and Mascot. (For a description of these roles, refer to Appendix III.)

If we are rational beings, why is it that many times, our body, near the point of collapse or exhaustion, has to tell our mind that we need to slow down, rather than our mind telling our body first? In my own case, I had a heart attack at age 34 before I began to make some changes in my lifestyle. And ironically, as I began to listen to and be more attuned to my body and its limitations, I began to listen to and be more attuned to my heart, to my feelings.

With his selective hearing, he picks up on certain Christian messages and then, as he does most things, carries it to an extreme. For example, telling this co-dependent, "lost Christian," that he should put himself last and remind him of the Scriptural passage "Thus the last shall be first and the first shall be last" (Matthew 20:16), gives him the authorization to go full steam ahead in this manner. At first, it seems to be a perfect fit, but as time goes by, he begins to take less and less responsibility for himself, and it becomes more and more painful. Concentrating on the other and ignoring himself, his identity slips away. As the son says about the father, Willie Loman, in *Death of a Salesman*, "He never knew who he was." But, by God, he's working out his salvation by being responsible for other people's salvation. The more he does, the better person, the better Christian, he thinks he is. Since his goal is to attain salvation, and since that is so closely tied to other people, he must control them for their salvation as well as his own. While on his teeter-totter, he's on the bottom and his neighbor, his brother, the other are high in the air above him. He must be doing the right thing, the Christian thing.

Finally, Melody Beattie has a poignant comment about responsibility and the Bible story of Mary and Martha. "While Mary sat and talked with Jesus and His friends, Martha cleaned and cooked. Before long, the story goes, Martha started banging pans, accusing Mary of being lazy. Martha complained that she had to do everything while Mary relaxed and enjoyed herself. Does this sound familiar? Jesus didn't let this one go by. He told Martha to hush. Mary knows what's important, He said. Mary made the right decision."[6]

Healing And Forgiveness. If we look at the gospels, one of the main actions of Jesus was healing bodies and souls. To be an instrument of healing and forgiveness is certainly a Christian goal. One of the roles that a "lost Christian" plays, especially in relationship to someone who has an addiction, is that of enabler. She wants to shield that person from the pain and negative consequences of the behavior. She wants to stop the other person's pain. But she accepts self-inflicted pain for a long time as well as other-inflicted pain.

She tries very hard to forgive others for their abuse, their weaknesses, their addictions, their sins, but finds it almost impossible to forgive herself for these same things. Somehow she just can't bring herself even to let God forgive her for them, either. Her sense of self-esteem is so low that she just doesn't seem to be worthy of it. Then she commits the same sin, makes the same mistakes, falls into the same patterns over and over and is thus plagued by guilt and shame. Harboring resentments and frustrations, she says that she forgives someone for what they have done or said, but the forgiveness has conditions. "I forgive you, but . . ." Then when the other person doesn't keep the condition or repeats the same behavior, the cycle begins again. And, she believes God acts this way too.

Going back to the Prayer of St. Francis at the beginning of this chapter, our "lost Christian" is trying to live it by consoling, pardoning, understanding the other, while crying out for these things for herself. Unable to express her needs or ask for help, she shelps along telling herself that it'll be better in heaven. But I read somewhere that the Kingdom of God is at hand! But not in the "lost Christian's" book.

Suffering And Death. When one looks for the ultimate symbol or sacramental of Christianity, inevitably it is the cross. This is the mechanism of Jesus redeeming us. The cross is synonymous with suffering and death. We use the phrase, "We all have our cross to bear," and that is certainly true. The co-dependent, non-recovering Christian is no stranger to suffering and pain, especially mental and emotional. He sees himself as a martyr, someone who is persecuted, unselfish and dedicated to helping mankind. However, he fails to realize that much of his pain comes from his efforts at "helping" (controlling and manipulating) other people. He feels that he's doing it for their own good as well as his own good. Remember he depends on them for affirmation, approval and his sense of self-worth instead of on himself.

But he's not willing to accept whatever they choose to do. Rather he must have input, sort of like telling someone how to adjust a mirror so he can see himself in it. This control of his reflection is paramount. And then of course there's the connection that he wins his salvation through helping other people win their salvation, whether they like it or not!

For some, their tolerance for pain and suffering is a measure of how good a job they're doing at being a Christian. They try to carry their cross joyfully but they don't mind telling you how bad they have it. It is rare that a dramatic sacrifice of one's life for Christianity occurs today in America, but the daily, small sacrifice of one's self occurs millions of times. Jesus' invitation to take up the cross and follow Him empowers many to endure all kinds of pain, some justified and some not. However, just experiencing pain and suffering does not mean that it is redemptive pain and suffering. Jesus said: "If a man wishes to come after me, he must deny his very self, take up his cross, and begin to *follow in my footsteps* (italics added). Whoever would save his life will lose it, but whoever loses his life *for my sake* (italics added) will find it." (Matthew 16:24-25) The "lost Christian" loses track of Jesus' footsteps and sets out on a new path of his own. He's suffering for his own sake, not Jesus' sake.

Resurrection. Jesus said "I am the resurrection and the life; whoever believes in me, though he should die, will come to life; and whoever is alive and believes in me will never die." (John 11:25-26) The Christian needs to internalize that the person of Jesus is a redemptive dynamic. The "lost Christian" sees Jesus as a means to an end. The Resurrection is out there somewhere, it's other-worldly, it's at the end of the rainbow. It has little to do with the here and now. There is no glory or joy now. But Jesus said: "You cannot tell by careful watching when the reign of God will come. Neither is it a matter of reporting that it is here or there. The reign of God is already in your midst." (Luke 17:20-21) Another translation states that the "Kingdom of God is within you."

The "lost Christian" cannot accept that. She believes that the focus is not only on the other person, but on the other world as well. It's easy to get confused because Jesus before Pilate said: "My kingdom does not belong to this world. If my kingdom were of this world, my subjects would be fighting to save me from being handed over to the Jews. As it is, my kingdom is not here." (John 18:36) But Jesus is indicating that His kingdom is non-militaristic and non-political. But it is certainly a reality *now* for the Christian. But the "lost Christian" fulfills the admonition of Jesus that ". . . Every kingdom divided against itself is laid waste. Any house torn by dissension falls." (Luke 11:17)

The "lost Christian" is as divided here as she is in Faith and Truth and Love (as we have seen in our earlier discussion). She says that she's saved — redeemed — but she doesn't act like it. She's too busy trying to be a savior or redeemer herself. She's actually in competition with Jesus for this title (not in any "women's lib" sense). Some would call it a "Messiah complex." But, in any case, it distorts, it divides, it causes anguish. The message of being saved and freed from the bondage of sin falls on the deaf ears of the "lost Christian."

Grace. Grace seems to be closely related to the concept of God's Will. As Christians we ask for the grace to *do* God's Will. We also have the belief that God never gives us more than we can handle. This can be a death wish for the non-recovering, co-dependent Christian. This allows him to accept any and all unhealthy relationships, crazy, and abusive situations, harmful people, and irresponsible behaviors. Instead of grace being the medium by which God works in and through me and other people, it becomes the motivation to accept anything and anyone that comes my way.

This certainly affects the "lost Christian's" free will, his sense of responsibility, his ability to love, his understanding of faith and truth, his capability of forgiving, and his participation in the Paschal Mystery. Instead of getting out of situations or relationships that are detrimental to one's health or even one's salvation, he can be sucked in by what he might feel is fate.

Rather than seeing the hand of God in his life, he might feel like he's under God's thumb. Life is an ordeal to be endured, rather than a gift to be embraced. Certainly we all have our ups and downs, our good days and our bad, but with the "lost Christian," viewing life as an ordeal is the standard operating procedure. His delusion of being so unselfish, dedicated and giving is debunked in his self-pity, his preoccupation, and his compulsion to remote-control his image through other people, as a puppeteer does by pulling on the strings of his dolls. Rather than hearing the melody of "Amazing Grace," the "lost Christian" echoes the sounds of "For Whom the Bell Tolls." On his ordination announcement card, a friend had printed, "The man whose Joy is Jesus can never be sad!" The thought rarely occurs to the person we've been describing. In fact, rather than the Gospel being the "Good News," he can more readily relate to it as "Bad News" because of the pain that he finds in trying to live the Christian message.

Mystery And Paradox. The last of our Scriptural mandates is mystery and paradox. Undoubtedly our Christian faith has many mysteries and many seeming contradictions that are difficult for anyone to accept. The "lost Christian," who is very much into control and manipulation, has even greater difficulty. She becomes her own worst enemy by constantly needing to understand and explain, while being short on acceptance and acknowledgment of serendipity. There is a fatalism that develops as she begins to feel locked into her particular situation and does not allow for growth, change or learning. She does not appreciate her particular, individual history and its role in God's plan. The sense of wonder or awe about life is missing and life becomes more plastic, sterile and numerical. Excitement, enjoyment, and happiness are missing from everyday life.

The expectation is that someday this will all be different. But someday never comes. We only have one shot at this life. As Father Joseph Gallagher says ". . . we don't solve our problems and then start living. We solve our problems by living."[7] Besides being called to strive for perfection, we are also called to accept imperfection in ourselves and in others. We make mistakes and need to learn from them.

All of the other mandates of Scripture have elements of mystery and paradox in them. Together, Faith, Truth, Love, Free Will, Responsibility, Healing and Forgiveness, Suffering and Death, Resurrection and Grace form the mosaic of our Christian faith. This paradigm or stereotype of a non-recovering, co-dependent Christian is very depressing and disheartening, as some of you know from your own lives. I have been to some of these places on this journey myself and have experienced others through relationships and the shared experience of others. But, now, I would like to take you to another stop on the journey toward recovery for the co-dependent Christian. Although this place is not without difficulties or pain, I have found it to be a much more positive and fulfilling place.

Reflection/Discussion Questions

How would you rate your self-esteem?

Can you relate to this "skewed" image of the Ten Christian Mandates? How? Which of them is your biggest problem?

Do you find yourself having "mixed feelings" about being a "good Christian?" What do you do with those feelings?

Do you, at times, feel worn out, empty, tired, burned out as a Christian?

Are you in a "helping" profession or job? If you relate to many of the co-dependent characteristics, did that plus your Christian upbringing help draw you to that job or career? Does this contribute to the conflict that you experience?

Do you find this conflict in certain areas (work, home, friends, Church, etc.) or in all aspects of your life?

Can you relate to any of the dysfunctional family roles in Appendix III?

What do you do to cope with unpleasant feelings? (Eat, work, exercise, gamble, use drugs/alcohol, etc.)

What one thing do you regret not doing in your life and why did you not do it?

What self-destructive behaviors do you do? What triggers them?

Name something that you hate to do, but do for others (name them)?

CHAPTER IV
The Recovering
Co-dependent Christian

Greatest Love Of All

. . . They can't take away my dignity.
Because, the greatest love of all is happening to me.
I found the greatest love of all inside of me.
The greatest love of all is easy to achieve,
Learning to love yourself is the greatest love of all.
. . . Find your strength in love.[1]

It is significant to me that I am not aware of a religious hymn or song that promotes love of self as this secular song does. Taken out of the context of the process presented here, this song might seem to be egotistical and self-centered. But in the discussion of the co-dependent Christian, I see it as a valuable message. For example, in the song's second stanza, there is a reference to a "hero." For the Christian, this hero is Jesus. The song also speaks about the necessity of learning love of self, and implies, to me, the way the socialization process has skewed that for the co-dependent Christian as we saw in Chapter II. But I believe that for the co-dependent Christian, learning to love himself is the key that unlocks the door. Once this door is opened, he can see the path much more clearly and no longer has to remain lost.

If I were to videotape myself or another non-recovering, co-dependent Christian as described in the previous two chapters, and take a snapshot of one of the scenes, and then ask, "What's wrong with this picture?" invariably the answer would be, a "lack of self-love." What can be done about this? How does one start from scratch after thirty, forty, fifty years of living? How can one change years of experience and well-developed habits? There are several things that need to be done.

I'm sure you've heard the old adage that admitting and acknowleding the problem is half the battle. The reason that is true in this case, as well as elsewhere, is that the person has begun to deal with his denial and has the courage to think positively about what steps to take to deal with the issue. Therefore, this is primary. It is necessary to recognize that there is a problem and it is helpful to be able to put a label of some kind on it so that the human mind-computer can begin to organize and understand information that is made available to it. For our purposes, that label is "I am co-dependent, AND I am Christian."

Secondarily, the recovering co-dependent Christian needs the seek balance in his life. Remember the image of the boy on the teeter-totter? Well, he can't always be on the bottom, nor can the other person always be on the bottom. To play the game as it's meant to be played, to have fun and enjoy it, both must take turns and sometimes the board is just level. We saw earlier that thinking and acting in extremes is a co-dependent characteristic. The middle ground should be considered. The Greeks called it, "nothing to excess." Today we say "too much of a good thing is not good." Moderation is a key issue for the recovering co-dependent Christian to bring to his self-concept, his relationships with others and his relationship with God.

Third, this individual needs to take time and put forth great effort to get to know and understand herself; her likes and dislikes; what she's good at and what she needs to work on; what she really feels about certain issues or situations or people. She needs to develop a true appreciation of herself for what she is, as well as an honest appraisal of herself as a Christian person. And she is not really starting from scratch. Rather, she needs to accentuate the positive aspects of her life and work on changing the negative ones in whatever situation she finds herself at the time her recovery process starts. She needs to begin that sabbatical of self-love that I talked about in the introduction. But, again the purpose is not to become introverted and continuously examine her own navel, but rather to get back on the path with God and others. It is better to take a detour, than to miss the road completely! And if one of the goals of this process is, as Shakespeare put it, "to thine ownself be true," one must be getting to know one's self during this journey we call life in order to know how to be true to that self.

A philosophical concept that needs to be implemented in this recovery process is to "question the question." This is a fourth requirement. Regardless of what one does, remember that there are always further questions that can be asked. For example, "Is this what I really think?"; "What is my true feeling about this?"; "Am I being honest?"; "Is this the most appropriate question for me to ask?"; "What is my motivation in this?" etc.

But again, the purpose of this is not to become a compulsive asker of questions, but rather to strive for awareness, growth and understanding of self and what has been missing from that self, contributing to this problem involving relationships. The co-dependent Christian needs to see himself as a blood relative of God (God's child); as a marvelous creature called a human being; and as a social, rational person. Asking questions can help tremendously in this endeavor, especially in trying to discern God's Will and in the imitation of Jesus.

From the time I was a young boy I remember having a triangular concept of relationships that has stayed with me the rest of my life, that is, an awareness of the need to have a good relationship with myself, with other people and with God. The intriguing thing about this is, not only that it imitates the relational aspect of the Trinity, namely Father, Son and Spirit; but also , that it is the core component of recovery from co-dependency, true love of self, of others and of God. The other noteworthy fact is that, despite knowing this intellectually, it had no deterring effect on my development of co-dependent behaviors.

This leads to a final requirement, changing one's behavior. Think back to our discussion of feelings following behavior, not waiting for feelings to change so the actions or behaviors will change. As with any other program of recovery from any other problem, addiction, etc., one must take action in order to change and to spark recovery. By *doing*, one can change and foster new feelings. Although attitude is important, one cannot *think* one's self into recovery or getting better. In this case, one must *do*. And expressing our feelings and changing our feelings is what we are trying to accomplish. Father Joseph Gallagher says, "I now believe that the only cure for bad feelings is good feelings, that only creative feelings can outwit destructive feelings, ... In fact, my vote would be that the curse of our age is a certain feelinglessness, a fear of deep, genuine and ample emotion."[2]

But how does this happen? How can one act in order to change feelings? John Bradshaw in his video series on Homecoming tells a beautiful story about the psychiatrist Karl Menninger. It seems that a wealthy family in the Midwest had tried to help their depressed mother with all kinds of therapeutic techniques and medications etc. to no avail. (Obviously a clinically depressed individual does not have a very good self-concept.) She had seen one therapist after another without success. After this had gone on for some time, they brought Dr. Menninger to see their mother. He spent about half an hour talking with her and he took note of two things: all the beautiful African violets she had in her home; and that she expressed a great interest in her church. Before leaving, Dr. Menninger's advice was for the woman to take note of any occasions at church such as weddings, baptisms, birthdays, funerals, etc. and to send those individuals one of her gorgeous African violets. In no time, she found a sense of purpose, made new friends, and was drawn out of herself, so that her depression disappeared. By doing, by action, her feelings of depression were changed to ones of belonging, of purpose and of friendship. A miracle? Perhaps. But, in its most basic form, this brilliant deduction was merely taking positive factors out of the present reality and channeling the emotion in a productive, constructive way. Assuming that the woman was a believer because her church was important to her, this activity had a significant positive impact on her relationship with God, on her self-concept, thus lifting her depression, and, on her relationships with other people.

For the "lost Christian" admitting the problem and beginning to confront the denial is the first step of the journey "of a hundred miles." Afer that, each of these other steps, as well as working on the denial, become a continuous life-long process to illuminate and discern the path. And just as we saw how a poor self-image is formed and shaped in the socialization dynamic, the recovering co-dependent Christian must assume responsibility for focusing, adjusting and reshaping his self-concept, his God-concept, and his other-concept. And although the self-concept is primary, the other two facets are intrinsically linked to the self. For, as we are told in Scripture, we see Jesus in the "least of the brethren" (other people) as well as in ourselves ["On that day you will know that I am in my Father, and you in me, and I in you." (John 14:20)] And whoever sees Jesus in turn sees the Father ["Believe me that I am in the Father and the Father is in me." (John 14:11)] It is a circular relationship.

What is the basis for this idea of the recovering co-dependent Christian? The life of Jesus. Jesus *is* the antithesis of a co-dependent. He also practiced what He preached! (Some might question this, believing that Jesus was the consumate co-dependent instead. They might argue that Jesus was so wrapped up in doing His Father's [the Other's] will, that He may well have lost Himself in the process! My view is that as the second person of the Trinity and as God, Jesus' development in His human consciousness was *self*-fulfilling rather than *other*-fulfilling — by being who He is(was), Jesus was accomplishing His mission as Son of God.)

Jesus was not a people pleaser, saying or doing things that others wanted to hear or see. The Jewish people of that time wanted a military leader who would lead a rebellion and overthrow the Romans. Jesus arrived as a helpless, dependent infant. He preached love, even love of your enemies and said His "Kingdom was not of this world." They wanted a king who would usher in an age of peace and prosperity. He said, "Do not suppose that my mission on earth is to spread peace. My mission is to spread not peace, but division . . . . Whoever loves father or mother, son or daughter, more than me is not worthy of me. He who will not take up his cross and come after me is not worthy of me." (Matthew 10:34, 37-38) They were wrapped up in legalistic jargon, externals, and some did things merely as a ritualistic show. But Jesus spoke about the "spirit of the Law" and stated that He came not to abolish the Law but to fulfill it. (Matthew 5:17-20) But (an example of the mystery and paradox present in Jesus' message) He also said that the old commandments of "an eye for an eye, and a tooth for a tooth," and "love your countryman but hate your enemy" were to be replaced by the Law of Love. (Matthew 5:38-48) They wanted a politician, someone with the "gift of gab," someone who could be an ambassador to the other cultures of their time. Jesus spent His time with the sinners, the poor, the lepers, the outcasts of His day, not the generals, the princes and kings. He was not into diplomacy. Rather, I would say, His was a grass roots movement.

Jesus was not one to bargain when people rejected Him or turned away. He wasn't afraid that people wouldn't like Him. Unlike a co-dependent person, Jesus did not fear rejection, but rather He expected it. When He sent His disciples out to the towns and villages, He told them to shake the dust from their feet if the people did not welcome them. (Luke 10:10-11) When the rich young man turned away after Jesus told him to sell all that he had and give it to the poor, Jesus didn't say, "No, wait! Don't go!" (Luke 18:18-24) He did not hesitate to "tell it like it is" with regard to the Pharisees and the scribes: "Woe to you scribes and Pharisees, you frauds! You are like white-washed tombs, beautiful to look at on the outside but inside full of filth and dead men's bones. Thus you present to view a holy exterior while hypocrisy and evil fill you within." (Matthew 23:27-29)

Jesus was radically different from the Messiah that the Jews expected, and both He and they had to get used to the idea.

Jesus shook the status quo down to its bedrock. As His self-awareness, His self-concept and His human consciousness unfolded in His own mind, He became more outspoken. But He was not some child prodigy who took the land by storm. No, other than the brief glimpse of Jesus as a boy of twelve amazing those teachers in the temple, we are told that "He went down with them then, and came to Nazareth, and was obedient to them. . . . Jesus, for his part, progressed steadily in wisdom and age and grace before God and men." (Luke 2:51-52) What do you suppose that Jesus did for those eighteen years until He began His public ministry at about the age of thirty? I suspect that He worked hard, prayed hard, played hard, studied, relaxed, and did the things that He liked to do as well as the things that He had to do. I think He took care of Himself and enjoyed His family and friends. I think He did His best at whatever He did. I think He wrestled with His self-concept and self-awareness and prayed for the Father's help while striving to do His Father's Will. His public ministry was a relatively short three years as compared to the thirty years of His "private ministry." He did not cut corners, but rather became a rabbi at about the customary time for His day, age thirty. He *gradually* matured and developed mentally, emotionally, spiritually and physically, as "the carpenter's son."

I see Jesus as using those eighteen years to His own advantage. I don't see Him as agonizing and counting down the years with hand wringing and anxiety attacks. I see Him as "letting go" and concentrating on doing the Will of God which, by the way, would require taking time for Himself. This would culminate in such things as His going off into the desert for forty days and not worrying, "Am I being selfish? Should I call the disciples now rather than waiting? What will they say or do without me?" He also went off to pray on several other occasions. He had to prioritize His actions and decide whether to preach, or heal, or pray, or rest, or fast, or party, or work, or visit family and friends. Just like you and I. He had to live in the present and not dwell on the past or be anxious about tomorrow. He had to take care of Himself. There's even a commandment that says so. The fifth: Thou shall not kill. I should know. I had to give a talk on it in front of the whole seventh grade class. What I remember was, that besides prohibiting murder and suicide, it promoted self care and preservation of life: eating right, exercising, getting rest, learning and growing.

It's amazing how you can find "new" things in Scripture even though you may have read through it several times over the years. That happened to me with the Gospel read at Mass recently. "The apostles returned to Jesus and reported to him all that they had done and what they had taught. He said to them, 'Come by yourselves to an out-of-the-way place and rest a little.' People were coming and going in great numbers, making it impossible for them to so much as eat. So Jesus and the apostles went off in the boat by themselves to a deserted place." (Mark 6:30-32) Never mind that this was the prelude to feeding the five thousand and the miracle of the loaves and the fish. The point is that Jesus saw the need for rest and recreation, taking time out from the busy day. Imagine that!

In all four Gospels the story of the anointing at Bethany appears: "When Jesus was in Bethany reclining at table . . . a woman entered carrying an alabaster jar of perfume made from expensive aromatic nard. Breaking the jar, she began to pour the perfume on his head. Some were saying to themselves indignantly: 'What is the point of this extravagant waste of perfume? It could have been sold for over three hundred silver pieces and the money given to the poor.' They were infuriated at her. But Jesus said: 'Let her alone. Why do you criticize her? She has done me a kindness. The poor you will always have with you and you can be generous to them whenever you wish, but you will not always have me. She has done what she could. By perfuming my body she is anticipating its preparation for burial. I assure you, wherever the good news is proclaimed throughout the world, what she has done will be told in her memory.' " (Mark 14:3-9) The *Jerome Biblical Commentary* states that although Jesus was not in favor

of extravagance, He graciously accepted the woman's generous gift. "[I]t is the only action in the Gospels that is promised
a perpetual and universal memory."[3]

Jesus was not passive or non-assertive. He did not always
turn the other cheek as He did during His Passion. He had
a sense of timing about His mission and the Father's will. He
had a sense of His rights as a person that could not be manipulated by an angry crowd of people, that He would not let be
manipulated. For example, there were at least two accounts
earlier in His public ministry when some of the Jews were ready
to kill Jesus. In His developing human consciousness, He might
have said, "Well, if I'm supposed to die anyway, I might as
well get this over with! Why bother with all the hoopla and
fanfare of riding into Jerusalem, etc. I'll just submit to the
wishes of the masses. So be it!" The one account is in Luke
4:28-30: "At these words the whole audience in the synagogue
was filled with indignation. They rose up and expelled him from
the town, leading him to the brow of the hill on which it was
built and intending to hurl him over the edge. But he went
straight through their midst and walked away." Then, the other
is in John 8:57-59: "At this the Jews objected: 'You are not
yet fifty!' How can you have seen Abraham?' Jesus answered
them: 'I solemnly declare it: before Abraham came to be, I
AM.' At that they picked up rocks to throw at Jesus, but he
hid himself and slipped out of the temple precincts." The first
thing that comes to mind is that if Jesus had some insight that
He was to die on a cross, not by stoning or being thrown off
a cliff, He resisted because the people were trying to change
His mission.

Peter was doing the same thing when Jesus told the disciples about the kind of death He would have to endure: "At
this, Peter took him aside and began to remonstrate with him.
'May you be spared, Master! God forbid that any such thing
ever happen to you!' Jesus turned on Peter and said, 'Get
out of my sight, you satan! You are trying to make me trip
and fall. *You are not judging by God's standards but by
man's.*' " [Italics added] (Matthew 16:22-23) Peter, the Rock,

was acting as a temptation to Jesus, trying to control and alter Jesus' understanding of His mission, so Jesus put him in his place and rebuked him. (Please refer to Appendix IV for differences between non-assertive, assertive and aggressive behavior.)

Jesus would also not let the opposite situation occur — that in a moment of exhuberance, He would be made king. After the miracle of the loaves and the fish, "When the people saw the sign he had performed they began to say, 'This is undoubtedly the Prophet who is to come into the world.' At that, Jesus realized that they would come and carry him off to make him king, so he fled back to the mountain *alone* (italics added)." (John 6:14-15) Wasn't this a good thing that the people wanted to do? But, it was not in keeping with Jesus' sense of His mission, and He would not be deterred.

Jesus was not manipulative or controlling, as a co-dependent person would be. He was a leader and a take-charge person. But He called the disciples to follow Him and it was up to them to decide. He invited; they had to respond. He did not force people to do things. He was not a rescuer or caretaker, volunteering to do for others what they should do for themselves. (What's that old saying, "God helps those who help themselves?") He required a response from the woman at the well, from Peter, from the other apostles, from Zacchaeus, from the centurion, etc. He cured the ill and the crippled, but they were brought to Him or came on their own and sought Him first.

Jesus did require a decision and a commitment. He would have subscribed to the modern-day saying, "Not to decide, is to decide." (The confession of sins at Mass says, "I have sinned . . . in what I have done, and in what I have failed to do . . . .") He told people to "Say, 'Yes' when you mean 'Yes' and 'No' when you mean 'No.' " (Matthew 5:37) Stanley and Brown in the *Jerome Biblical Commentary*, when speaking about St. John's Gospel, state: "In John's eyes, no man can afford to remain indifferent to Jesus: Everyman must declare himself for Jesus or against him."[4]

Jesus, we are told, was like us in all things except sin. Yet He seemed to have a good grasp of His emotions. Unlike a co-dependent person, the evangelists portray Jesus as someone who felt His feelings and expressed them. We see Him get angry at the money changers in the Temple, turning over their tables and spilling their coins in the process; we watch His compassion for His hosts in responding to His mother's request at the wedding in Cana; we hear Him weep over the city of Jerusalem; we see His mercy in healing and in forgiving sins; we see His marvelous creativity in all the parables He told. And we see Jesus weep for His friend Lazarus, and *then* He raised him from the dead. Jesus entered into the moment, felt the loss and the sadness *first*, and then performed the miracle. He did not say something shallow like, ''Don't worry, he's not really dead!'' Of course, we feel His unconditional love that has no strings attached, but does not force one to embrace it. We see His agony in the garden prior to His capture, when He must have felt let down and almost abandoned by His Father and His friends: ''He said to his disciples, 'Stay here while I go over there and pray.' He took along Peter and Zebedee's two sons, and began to experience sorrow and distress. Then he said to them, 'My heart is nearly broken with sorrow. Remain here and stay awake with me.' He advanced a little and fell prostrate in prayer. 'My Father, if it is possible, let this cup pass me by. Still, let it be as you would have it, not as I.' When he returned to his disciples, he found them asleep. He said to Peter, 'So you could not stay awake with me for even an hour? Be on guard, and pray that you may not undergo the test. The spirit is willing but nature is weak.' Withdrawing a second time, he began to pray: 'My Father, if this cannot pass me by without drinking it, your will be done!' Once more, on his return, he found them asleep; they could not keep their eyes open. He left them again, withdrew somewhat, and began to pray a third time, saying the same words as before. Finally he returned to his disciples and said to them: 'Sleep on now. Enjoy your rest! The hour is on us when the Son of Man is to be handed over to the power of evil men.' '' (Matthew 26:36-45)

Why do you suppose the evangelist included the details about this account? We're not looking at the Six Million Dollar Man or the Incredible Hulk here! This was a feeling, loving, hurting human being they were describing. His best friends weren't giving Him much support, He was scared, frightened and anxious, and perhaps somewhat sarcastic when He told them to "Sleep on now. Enjoy your rest!" He could have copped a resentment against Peter and said, "Ok, that's it! You're not going to lead My Church!" (Not to mention the triple denial) Although His entire life was leading up to this moment, the Passion, Death and Resurrection, He still had doubts, fears and the slim hope that perhaps He didn't really have to go through all this. Maybe there would be a reprieve at the last minute like Abraham with Issac! The next question is, "If the God-man Jesus Christ experienced this range of emotion and was in touch with it in his humanity, why am I not allowed to experience *my* emotions?" Obviously, not only am I allowed, but I *must* if I am to claim to be human! I am not called to be a high gloss, plastic facade or a cardboard imitation. On a small card that a previous owner had glued to the inside of the door of the medicine cabinet in the bathroom of our house, I found this little ditty:

He was a very cautious man,
He never romped or played.
He never smoked, he never drank,
Nor ever kissed a maid.
And when he up and passed away
Insurance was denied.
For since he hadn't ever lived
They claimed he never died.

This certainly could not be said about Jesus. I believe that He lived life to the full, with gusto and zest. My image is that Jesus would have enjoyed commiserating with Zorba the Greek and Eleanor Roosevelt and Tevye of *Fiddler on the Roof* fame.

And there's more about the humanity of Christ that needs to be said. Jesus was tempted by the devil in the desert, but the mere temptation did not constitute sin. (Matthew 4:1-11) In the eyes of most people of His time, Jesus was a miserable failure. He certianly could not be considered a model of success. But as Mother Teresa responded to an interviewer who saw the squalor and poverty and illness of the people with whom she was working, "We are not called to be successful, but to be faithful." Jesus was single-minded in attempting to understand His vocation and in doing the Will of the Father. He was totally committed and faithful to that pursuit. Jesus was frustrated by the slowness of the disciples to really believe as evidenced by this passage from Matthew 17:16-18 in which a possessed boy is brought to Jesus: " 'I have brought him to your disciples but they could not cure him.' In reply Jesus said: 'What an unbelieving and perverse lot you are! How long must I remain with you? How long can I endure you? Bring him here to me.' " A Biblical commentary states that Jesus' words seem to refer "to the disciples who have failed in the use of the power that Jesus communicated to them."[5] But the note in the *New American Bible* states that the human Jesus was even a little co-dependent! "The disciples' failure to effect a cure seems to reflect unfavorably on Jesus. In response, he exposes their lack of trust in God and scores their neglect of prayer, i.e., of the conscious reliance on God's power when acting in Jesus' name."

Jesus was also limited by His humanity, by His personhood, by time, and by space. By being born a Jew, He could not be Roman or Greek. By living in Israel, He was not in the Orient or in the Americas. By being male, He was not female. By being a carpenter, He was not a merchant. He was born into a specific family, in a particular town, and in a certain socio-economic status. By virtue of His situation and circumstances, as well as by choices that He made, Jesus was limited.

And He also had a sense of the timing of His mission. Besides going through the usual preparation to be a rabbi, He saw a gradual development in His mission. At times He wanted His deeds and message to be shouted from the hilltops as when He told the messenger from John the Baptist: " 'Go back and report to John what you hear and see: the blind recover their sight, cripples walk, lepers are cured, the deaf hear, dead men are raised to life and the poor have the good news preached to them.' " (Matthew 11:4-5) Yet at other times, when the moment was not quite ready or opportune "he gave them strict orders not to tell anyone about him" (Mark 8:30) and after the transfiguration, "he strictly enjoined them not to tell anyone what they had seen, before the Son of Man had risen from the dead." (Mark 9:9)

It is this human Jesus, who was in touch with his emotions and expressed them, who had relationships with other people and with His Father, and who lived an authentic life, that I must use as my guide on the journey from *functioning* as a non-recovering, co-dependent Christian to *becoming* a recovering, co-dependent Christian. Over the years I have compared myself unfairly to a lot of people by choosing *only* their strong points, the things I admired about them or that attracted me toward them, and judging those against my totality — all my points, both strong and not so strong — and working myself into a hole when I fell short in the match up. Now I take comfort in knowing that there are only two comparisons I need make: one compares *myself* to *myself* so I can measure my progress in areas that I am working on; the second is that between myself and Jesus, and in that comparison, not only I, but *everyone* else, falls short. However, I see my goal as trying to imitate Christ as best as I possibly can. And even in this painful problem of co-dependency, Jesus shows me the way.

The institutional Catholic Church took initial steps in aiding its members in this process with the Second Vatican Council in the early sixties. One image that was used in describing the effects of the Council on the Catholic Church was that of "opening a window to let in fresh air" after centuries of being closed up and stale. There was a de-focusing on structure and the pyramidal image that had the pope and the college of cardinals at the top and the laity at the bottom. We could now call the "Church" *all* the "people of God," not only including the lay people, but especially counting the lay people. There was less emphasis on legalism such as abstaining from meat on Fridays and an overnight fast prior to receiving the Eucharist. In fact, these Church laws were removed. Fasting and penance were encouraged and recommended, but basically were left up to the individual's free will. There was a de-emphasis on legalism and dependence, and a greater promotion of freedom, independence and choice. The primacy of the individual's conscience was acknowledged, provided that person had a correctly formed conscience. [This seems to be a "gray area," determining if one's conscience is correctly formed. The need for balance is once again evident. Borrowing from Scott Peck, two extremes present themselves: "When neurotics are in conflict with the world they automatically assume that they are at fault. When those with character disorders are in conflict with the world they automatically assume the world is at fault."[6] Perhaps these two parameters delineate the middle ground of a sense of right and wrong, guilt and responsibility. I would venture to say that the "lost Christian" often does not have a correctly formed conscience and that is one of the "lost Christian's" major problems — internalizing the guilt, blame and shame that often are not justified.]

There was a major change in the ability to communicate especially at liturgy because the language of the people, the vernacular, could now be used instead of Latin. And there was a much greater emphasis on the human element such as different genre of music besides organ; an awareness that you were in church with other people; and that you could actually communicate with and touch them at the kiss of peace! The Sacrament of Penance or Confession became the Sacrament of Reconciliation or Healing. There was also the option of confessing to a priest face to face, allowing for the human interaction of senses and facial expression. And the Last Rites or Extreme Unction, an anointing prior to death, became the Anointing of the Sick, not just those on their death bed. But as more of the recovery process is embraced by individual "people of God" so too the Church will become more human, more authentic, more Christ-like, more ecumenical. So each individual who finds that this label of "non-recovering, co-dependent Christian" fits, has work to do.

As mentioned, one of the big non-recovery messages that I struggled with had to do with being humble. One of the tasks for the Christian who is searching to find the path is to develop a sense of true humility. Father Joseph Gallagher has good insight into this when he says, "A truly humble person doesn't think little of himself, rather he thinks of himself little." He goes on to give a definition that "Humility . . . is the willingness to be what you are and to do what you can." He concludes, "I am not God. These are the facts. The question is: Am I willing to be what I am?"[7] Father John Powell, S. J., speaks about humility and pride as having the same source, self-acceptance and self-appreciation of "realizing and savoring one's own goodness. Then virtue and vice part company. Pride claims this goodness and giftedness as personal accomplishment. Pride listens for applause, sniffs for incense. Pride is lonely without recognition and reward. Humility quietly knows that 'I have nothing which I was not given.' Humility is grateful, not grasping."[8]

This re-focusing is what the "found Christian," the recovering co-dependent Christian, needs to do. He needs to give thanks and glory to God for being himself! You've probably seen the poster, "God doesn't make junk!" Indeed He does not. He is the Supreme Artist and YOU are His prize work of art! Take pride in that and in *yourself*! But . . . also be grateful and truly humbled by it.

Another of those mainline messages that got misspoken by non-recovering, co-dependent Christians who may have been parents, teachers, priests or ministers and were misinterpreted or misconstrued by other young "lost Christians" like myself was the one about loving your neighbor as yourself. Indeed this is supposed to be an equation, and as in math, that means that what is on one side is equal to what is on the other side. If you weighed them, they should balance. The time, effort, energy, exhuberance, delight, commitment, pain, etc. spent on loving the other, needs to be equally spent on loving yourself. *Just as much*. No more, no less. The "found Christian" needs to develop a true sense of self love. In order to give of oneself, there must be something to give, namely a *self*, a sense of identity and personhood. In order to give love, one must be loved and thus have love to give. One must first possess a gift before sharing it with another. One must experience love, not just God's unconditional love, but also the true love *of* others and *by* others, as well as a true, unconditional love of one's self. For better or for worse, like it or not, this is the only self that we've got to deal with in this lifetime. As our song reads, "learning to love yourself is the greatest love of all."

Just as a therapist is expected to undergo therapy herself in order to deepen her self-understanding, her self-awareness, knowledge of her biases and weaknesses, as well as that of her strengths, so that she is better able to serve and help her clients, so too, the "found Christian" must engage in this strange activity of being self-centered and self-focused for this same purpose but in the balance and harmony of the circular relationships with God and others. Carl Jung is said to have been reflecting on the words of Jesus: "Whatever you do to the least of my brethren, you do unto me." Then Jung asks a very probing question: 'What if you discovered that the least of the brethren of Jesus, the one who needs your love the most, the one that you can help the most by loving, the one to whom your love will be most meaningful — what if you discovered that this least of the brethren of Jesus . . . is you?'[9] It is necessary for the "found Christian" to come to this insight and to act on it.

One of the rules of the dysfunctional family is "Don't Trust," as we saw in Chapter II. We also discussed how this affected faith and belief in God. This is perhaps its most devastating impact. A major aspect of the "found Christian's" journey is to renew both his faith in God and his faith in himself. Some might say, "I have never believed in myself! What do you mean 'renew' faith in myself!'' ''And as for my faith in God, well it's never been stronger! He's helping me through this!'' I would say to that person that he needs to look at the situation once again. Faith in God *must* carry over to faith in one's self. It has to. For I am a child of this God, made in His own image and likeness. The fact that I might feel this alienation from myself is a major symptom of the problem. St. Iranaeus said that the glory of God is man fully alive! And Jesus Himself told the disciples ''You are the light of the world. A city set on a hill cannot be hidden. Men do not light a lamp and then put it under a bushel basket. They set it on a stand where it gives light to all in the house. In the same way, your light must shine before men so that they may see goodness in your acts and give praise to your heavenly Father.'' (Matthew 5:14-16) And in the parable of the silver pieces or talents (Matthew 25:14-30), we see that the master (Jesus) does not want a one for one return on his money, but rather wants it to be multiplied and leaves it up to the individual servant's creativity as to how best to do this.

Obviously burying one's talents or covering up one's light does not fit in with God's plan for us. It is much more difficult for the ''lost Christian,'' who is constantly struggling to control and manipulate others into reflecting a certain image of himself, to find his true reflection in the Father, than it is for the ''found Christian,'' who is in the process of adjusting and focusing the lens of faith and the mirror of self-image, to find himself as a reflection and likeness of the Father. Trust in God and trust of one's self is essential.

The ''Don't Talk'' rule applies to communication with other people. We saw earlier how that dynamic operates. For the co-dependent Christian who is in the process of finding himself through a recovery effort, communicating with others is vitally important. Just because relationships have been difficult for this individual in the past, does not mean that he now becomes a recluse or a hermit, refusing to deal with people at all costs. Rather, the focus must be taken off other people and their role must be put in perspective. The ''lost Christian'' does not get better in a vacuum, but by using friends, family, counselor or therapist as a sounding board to do some of that reality testing that was squelched in growing up.

From the extreme of Sartre's view that "Hell is other people" to the echoes of the "Me Generation," we, as social beings, must come to grips with the fact that, as Father Joseph Gallagher states, other people are both part of our problem as well as part of our solution. He continues, "Our human choice, then, is not between pain and no pain, but between the pain of loving and the pain of not loving."[10] We get suport from other people, valuable feedback, love, a sense of ourself and a sense of relationship. Jesus could have said that "Whenever you (singular) are at prayer, I am with you." (In effect, He did say that.) But He made a point of saying, ". . . if two of you join your voices on earth to pray for anything whatever, it shall be granted you by my Father in heaven. Where two or three are gathered in my name, there am I in their midst." (Matthew 18:19-20) Community. Relationship. Sharing. Service. These are all integral elements of the Christian message as well as desirable values for a co-dependent person. But we must keep in mind the five recovery principles from the beginning of this chapter.

Mixed messages have been given and received. The truth must be sorted out, not just Christian Truth, but also Truth in one's own individual existence. Father John Powell, S. J. says that "We are as sick as we are secret."[11] The things about ourselves, about others, and about our relationships that we choose to ignore, to deny, to allow to imprison ourselves, are the things that make us sick. In the Adult Children of Alcoholics [& Other Dysfunctional Families] (ACoA) self-help groups as well as in Alcoholics Anonymous (AA), Narcotics Anonymous (NA), Alanon, etc., the "secret" is the addiction, the abuse, the chronic illness — whatever it is that magnetizes the family's energy around itself and will make the family seemingly look bad to outsiders. To the co-dependent Christian the secret can be the controlling, the manipulating, the people-pleasing, the doing "Christian acts," but not feeling "Christian feelings.'' (Whitewashed tombs?) As humans, we can give emphasis to something in two ways: taking about it all the time, or not talking about it at all. It is imperative for the ''found Christian'' to talk, to share, to be, with himself, his brothers and sisters, and His God.

I remember participating in a group facilitator's workshop several years ago. Part of the training, of course, was to actually experience a group setting each day over the five day period. It was about into the third day, I think, after two of the participants had kind of wrapped up their issues, that the facilitator was looking for someone else who had some ''work'' to do. I thought I was going to die! I felt like I was either going to swallow my heart or it was going to jump out of my chest! The fear and anxiety that I might be the next person to be asked to share my feelings, to deal with my feelings, and take the risk of revealing myself in a very personal way and asking for help, was almost overwhelming. I mean, I could empathize and listen and give feedback and relate to someone else talking about their problems ''until the cows came home.'' But *me*, talk about *my* feelings! Mr. Perfect! Mr. Control! I didn't have problems, *exactly*, and I didn't have feelings, *exactly*. I was secret and I was sick. But that is changing. By giving myself permission to talk, to share, to feel and to express myself, I am a better person today than I was then.

The third primary message to the non-recovering co-dependent Christian is ''Don't Feel.'' And this is perhaps the most devastating rule because of what it does to one's self-esteem, and one's ability to relate to others and to God. What can one do to counteract this ingrained message? As the leader said in my outpatient co-dependency recovery program, ''The healing is in the feeling.'' We must try to remember as many of those forgotten, repressed feelings from the past — many going back to childhood — as we can, and try to begin to identify feelings that we are having now, in the present. It seems awkward. It seems strange. It's painful. But it is necessary. Many of us are afraid of feeling. But as Joe S. says in *Out of Hell*, ''Just facing a fear . . . without doing some emotional work around the past and the fear's genesis, is quite analogous to pulling a weed out by the top. If you don't get the roots, it will grow back again, and again, and again . . ."[12] And chances are if I have a feeling whose intensity does not fit the present situation, I'm probably reacting to some incident from my past. Old buttons are being pushed; old feelings are surfacing.

We must try to be aware of our feelings and to accept them. We must counteract the old signs that feelings are sinful or harmful or bad. There was a television commercial that ran a few years ago that showed a mechanic at a garage with a car on a tow truck as he smirked, "You can pay me now, or pay me later." The implication was that one could do regular maintenance such as oil changes and pay a small price over time, or let things go too long, and ruin the engine, and pay a big price all at once. The same can be true with the firm, rigid control of emotion. Father Joseph Gallagher states: "To the degree that a man consciously or unconsciously resents and rejects his emotionality, he will be alienated from himself and from others."[13] Sound familiar? By not taking the risk of expressing emotion throughout our lives, we ignore the "routine maintenance " of being human, and thus, when we do pay, we pay long and hard as we come to the frustrating realization of being trapped inside ourselves and in Saran-wrapped relationships. All the time spent trying to take care of other people, and to be liked, and make them happy, while glossing over our own needs, has a horrible payback when we come to stark realization that we're not sure who we really are! It was wise Abe Lincoln who said you "can fool some of the people some of the time, and can even fool all of the people some of the time, but [you] can't fool all the people all the time." And in his song "Garden Party," Ricky Nelson sang "Learned my lesson well, can't please everyone, so you gotta please yourself."

We must allow ourselves to have our feelings, we must accept our feelings, and we must decide how we're going to act based on those feelings. I don't mean that we should not consider reason as well. Of course we should take other factors into consideration, such as common sense, the importance of the issue to ourselves and other people, the risks involved and the benefits. It can be very counterproductive to make each and every feeling into an "issue." However, that might be "just what the doctor ordered," so to speak, if that is the action that will begin to change our feelings about ourselves. Again in *Out of Hell*, Joe S. states "The feelings hold the power. And you need to take the power back if you're tired of co-dependent puppet-hood. . . . [T]hat power is the key to freedom."[14]

When thinking of emotions that have a negative connotation, I think of anger as one of the biggies. Why is this so? It can lead to arguments, violence, and sin. It is an emotion that is full of power. Yet we see Jesus fashion a whip and chase animals out of the temple, and overturn the tables of the moneychangers. (John 2:14-17) (We Christians cite this instance as the classic example of "justifiable" anger. In other words, Jesus had every right to be angry and He had every right to express His anger. Don't we at times have every right to be angry and have every right to express our anger?!) Jesus also "turned on Peter" and called him, "you Satan." (Matthew 16:23) And I don't exactly picture Jesus speaking in a soft whisper when he rebuked the Pharisees and called them "whitewashed tombs!"

But, on the other hand, keeping in mind the mystery and paradox in the Christian message, Jesus also says, "everyone who grows angry with his brother shall be liable to judgment; . . . If you bring your gift to the altar and there recall that your brother has anything against you, leave your gift at the altar, go first to be reconciled with your brother, and then come and offer your gift." (Matthew 5:22, 23-24) And St. Paul seems to be on the same track when he says, "If you are angry, let it be without sin. The sun must not go down on your wrath; do not give the devil a chance to work on you." (Ephesians 4:26-27) The message does not seem to be, "Keep your anger inside," but rather, "Express your anger, get it out, but do not dwell on it or be consumed by it.'' There is not much that can compare with the imprisoning slavery of hatred, anger and resentment. Maybe that's why self-help programs and the Twelve Steps tell us to pray for the person we hate or resent or are angry with. Maybe that's why Jesus calls us to love our enemies, because in the mystery of opposites, we are set free by such a change in our behavior. We then get the weight off our chest and are free of the other's domination. And furthermore, if the anger does not get expressed, it stays inside to boil, and seethe, and fester while making the individual more and more depressed, and reducing one's level of effectively living a Christian life to a great extent. This is not what I would consider to be God's Will for me!

In talking about anger and resentment, Joe S. says, ''Praying away the resentment was extremely important. However, so was venting the anger. They're different. Some people in self-help don't know that. The resentment is the recurring get-even thoughts that lead to a kind of paralyzing brain cancer after a while. Anger is a feeling, that when affected, needs to be expressed somehow. Whether to the source, sympathetic friends, or in the car with the windows rolled up — or down.''[15]

Dr. Theodore Rubin, author of *The Angry Book*, states ''I believe you either feel all your feelings or eventually none at all. You cannot select which feelings you will feel and which you won't . . . . Negate anger, and you also negate love.''[16] I think Jesus understood this. I think He chose the disciples because of their passion, their humanity and the fire in their hearts. He knew this was not a job for whimps! There's a poem by William Blake that goes: ''I was angry with my friend: I told my wrath, my wrath did end . . . I was angry with my foe: I told it not, my wrath did grow.''

Jesus also tried to bring balance into play and take the focus off ''the other'' and put it on ''the self.'' ''If you want to avoid judgment, stop passing judgment. Your verdict on others will be the verdict passed on you. Why look at the speck in your brother's eye when you miss the plank in your own? How can you say to your brother, 'Let me take that speck out of your eye,' while all the time the plank remains in your own? You hypocrite! Remove the plank from your own eye first; then you will see clearly to take the speck from your brother's eye.'' (Matthew 7:1-5) And earlier, Jesus said that deeds of mercy should be kept secret and, when giving alms, the left hand should not know what the right hand is doing. (Matthew 6:3-4)

And there is a need for balance and restraint with our emotions, too. A nuclear reaction gone wild is a bomb; in check, the reactor produces energy and power. Water running rampant is a flood or typhoon; harnessed, it, too, generates power. Fire burning wildly is destructive, but controlled, it is useful and produces heat. And when we "have a handle" on our emotions and express them, we are passionate, energetic leaders who thrive on life. There is a happy median between being overly explosive and unhealthily repressive of our emotions, our energy producers. We must begin living in the realm of *all* our emotions, for this is our nature. To be human is to feel. Except for reason, what else is there that separates us from other animals but our range of emotions?

And then there is love. Once again, Father Joseph Gallagher comes right to the point: ". . . all of us are people who need people. Yet one of the most illuminating indicators of the human condition, of man's predicament and plight and fractured status is that many of us find it so hard to discover what love really is, and so hard to practice what love really means, and so afraid of what love really does. It couldn't be stranger if fish were afraid of water and eagles were frightened by the open sky."[17]

Love is the answer to life's Jeopardy question. But what *is* the question? What do we as persons, what do we co-dependent Christians, want more than anything? To love and to be loved. But is this even possible? Of course it is! Granted, this has not been our forte in the past, but after beginning to utilize a recovery format, we cannot lose sight of the very reason we need this Christian co-dependency recovery in the first place! Nor can we go back to our old, unhealthy habits that we've been struggling to outgrow. Love is balanced in the middle range. When we are free — to truly be ourselves and to be comfortable with that — we will be able to love like we never thought posible. By re-thinking our focus and perspective, by changing our behavior in order to feel different toward ourselves, others and even God, if need be, this *is* possible. To change is not easy, but the pain is too great not to change. Plus there is hope for a better, fuller, more authentic life!

For the "found Christian," love does not become a totally introspective, selfish endeavor. Recovery's purpose is not to impress other people, to go on an ego trip, or to become narcissistic. Indeed the focus of love does need to turn to the other, but only when balanced by love for myself. Melody Beattie says, "We're all working with approximately the same material — humanity. It's how we feel about ourselves that makes the difference. It's what we tell ourselves that makes the difference."[18] The time for the negative, critical messages to ourselves is over! The time for positive, loving, supportive messages is now! (For example, in Co-Dependents Anonymous and Adult Children of Alcoholics self-help groups one of the recovery tools is to give one's self positive affirmations to reinforce love, encouragement, acceptance, support — the kind of messages that have been lacking in our lives, the kind of messages that we should have gotten from parents, friends, teachers, clergy, etc., but never did.)

One of the greatest positive, loving, supportive messages that I can give myself is that I am a beautiful child of God and God loves me. No hitches, no catches, no strings! I need to believe that and I need to hear that . . . from myself to myself. Just as the Golden Rule states, "Do unto others as you would have them do unto you," I believe we need to "Do unto ourselves as God does to us — He loves us!" It's OK to believe it and feel it!

In the Old Testament when asked His name by Moses, God replied, I AM WHO I AM. (Exodus 3:14) I believe that God's message to me is BE WHO I AM, or in the second person, BE WHO YOU ARE! As Christian co-dependents we become so wrapped up in the other that it seems as though our salvation, our vocation, and our happiness are there, outside ourselves. But I believe that God does not call me to be someone I'm not, but rather invites me on that journey inward, to "inner space" as Dag Hammerskjold called it, to discover, to actualize my potential, to develop, to become ME! To look in the mirror is to see the reflection of God. And I am unique, right down to my fingerprints! I am most God-like when I am myself. Because that is my calling, that is my vocation, that is God's Will for me. I can rejoice in just Being! I don't have to do, or earn or deserve or play a particular role. However, in being myself I will invariably demonstrate and manifest my *being* through my acting.

This is not to say that I am perfect. Far from it. (But neither is anyone else.) But in acknowledging my sinfulness, my weakness and my defects, I can, in true humility, offer my totality to God because I am loved and I am saved. So although my life has been shaped and formed as a co-dependent person, my life has also been changed and transformed by redemption through Jesus Christ. That is the Good News!

In today's self-help, recovery jargon there is talk of needing to re-parent ourselves and healing the "inner child" because of what was lacking in our childhoods as we grew up. Many of these things center around the issues that were examined in our discussion of the socialization process. Likewise I believe that a case can be made for a need to re-Christianize or re-Church ourselves because of what was lacking in our early understanding of our faith and the way it was taught as well as the messages that were taught to us. Just as we can learn to counteract our old co-dependent behaviors, we can learn to counteract our old "Christian" behaviors, the ones that have an unhealthy, stifling outcome, make us feel alienated from ourselves, our fellow humans, and our Creator, and keep us from experiencing the Kingdom on earth.

And speaking of the "inner child" and the need to re-parent ourselves, our parental images, if they were not healthy and wholesome, need to be re-established, but this time with the loving God of our recovery in mind. And when we look at Jesus' thoughts about children, we discover something interesting. The simplicity, the innocence, the trust, the purity, the honesty, the humility and the beauty of a child all are manifest. "On one occasion Jesus spoke thus: 'Father, Lord of heaven and earth, to you I offer praise; for what you have hidden from the learned and the clever you have revealed to the merest children.' (Matthew 12:25) At another time there was a discussion about ambition: "Just then the disciples came up to Jesus with the question, 'Who is of greatest importance in the kingdom of God?' He called a little child over and stood him in their midst and said: 'I assure you, unless you *change* (italics added) and become like little children, you will not enter the kingdom of God. Whoever makes himself lowly, becoming like this child, is of greatest importance in that heavenly reign.' " (Matthew 18:1-4) In a third instance, ". . . children were brought to him so that he could place his hands on them in prayer. The disciples began to scold them, but Jesus said, 'Let the children come to me. Do not hinder them. The kingdom of God belongs to such as these.' And he laid his hands on their heads before he left that place." (Matthew 20:13-15) Jesus sets up the image of a child as a desirable model for His followers to imitate, even as adults. My guess is that Jesus was saying that if one does not possess those child-like qualities, one should attempt to develop them, or search for them in one's past, or even nurture them out of one's past, maybe by re-parenting!

And perhaps the culmination of all this comes in the story of Nicodemus. "A certain Pharisee named Nicodemus, a member of the Jewish Sanhedrin, came to him at night. 'Rabbi,' he said, 'we know you are a teacher come from God, for no man can perform signs and wonders such as you perform unless God is with him.' Jesus gave him this answer: 'I solemnly assure you, no one can see the reign of God unless he is begotten from above.' 'How can a man be born again once he is old?' retorted Nicodemus. 'Can he return to his mother's womb and be born over again?' Jesus replied: 'I solemnly assure you, no one can enter into God's kingdom without being begotten of water and Spirit. Flesh begets flesh, Spirit begets spirit. Do not be surprised that I tell you that you must all be begotten from above. The wind blows where it will. You hear the sound it makes but you do not know where it comes from, or where it goes. So it is with everyone begotten of the Spirit.' '' (John 3:1-8) Although the image of new birth and the water of baptism are old concepts, it may be more than just coincidence that Jesus points out that all Christians are in need of being born again. This may relate closely to the co-dependent Christian's need to re-learn and to re-experience some elements of our faith as transformed into behavior, as well as some developmental aspects of our family histories.

Jesus could have said that we need to start over, or repent, or make a new beginning. But He said we needed to be "born again," to epitomize that newness and freshness of a child; to either re-capture what we once had, or to capture it for the very first time if we have never possessed it. We need to bring that wonderful, free, loving child into reality in order to rid ourselves of our co-dependent baggage and our misguided Christian conduct. We need to give new birth to that child within us! We need to be "born again" in the Spirit!

So WHO is it that we've been talking about here? Us. You and me — each of us who can identify with the label of being both co-dependent *and* Christian. We need to change our attitude toward ourselves. When we look at that six-inch-tall glass with three inches of water in it, do we see it as half full or half empty? Do we know our stress points and stress signs — what they are and what they mean for us? For example, what does it mean when our mind starts racing, or when we start to obsess, or use drugs or alcohol, or get stomach pains and headaches, or feel depressed? What does it mean when we can't sleep, or want to lash out at other people, or are distracted in prayer (or don't pray period)? Do we feel that we're pessimistic, optimistic, or realistic about life? And what do each of these terms mean to us? For me, I need to give myself permission to do a heavenly balancing act or tightrope walk — to reach for the stars in my idealism, but to keep my feet on the ground in my practicality!

If I am 5'2" tall chances are I will not play center in the National Basketball Association. If I have little interest in biology and chemistry and can't stand the sight of blood, chances are I will not become a brain surgeon. If I'm in poor physical health, chances are I will not qualify to be a pilot. But if I really want to, I can reach for the stars and accomplish many things I set out to do. The ostrich is the largest living bird, but it can't fly! (I can just see an ostrich talking to God about this — "But you see, God , birds are supposed to fly, right?") But it can run very fast, up to 40 mph! It probably doesn't take an ostrich long to realize that it can't fly, but it might take it a while to realize that it can really run. On the other hand, a bumble bee is not supposed to be able to fly. Aerodynamically, it's wings are supposed to be too small to be able to support its body weight in flight. But, in these two examples, and I'm sure there are hundreds more, someone forgot to tell God! And I think that some of us are ostriches and some of us are bumble bees. Remember, with God, all things are possible. In recovery, pessimism and fatalism won't do. I need to give myself permission to succeed!

Another nature example that fits is the metamorphosis, the dramatic change of form and structure, of the caterpillar to the butterfly. To see this crawling, slow, worm-like creature it's hard to believe that it is transformed into a swift, graceful, flying burst of color! But it is merely realizing its potential and becoming what God meant it to be. We caterpillars need to see the butterflies within us! The potential and the beauty and the love are within us. We have to trust God and the process enough to let it materialize.

Certainly one of the major goals of this process is to grow in self-knowledge so that I can be a better person and so I can be the *best* me that I can be. The common denominator of our humanity is great enough that we have more similarities than we have differences. Therefore, self-knowledge leads to other-knowledge. This helps us in relationships. This also helps those of us who are in the helping professions. As one friend has said to me, we can only take others as far as we ourselves have gone. And similarly, another friend has remarked about the saying, "When the pupil is ready, the teacher will appear."

WHAT needs to happen now? Action. This entire process has been predicated on the need for action to come first in order to change our feelings about ourselves. The action can be divided into six parts. There is no particular order in which these steps need to be taken, and any one of them can be the entrance point into the recovery dynamic. But all of them can certainly yield positive results in the "found Christian's" journey.

Part one is prayer and spiritual direction. Through one's relationship with God in prayer and/or through the direction of one's pastor, minister, clergyperson or religious, we might become aware of a lack of identity, fulfillment, or self-esteem that plagues us in this conflict of being both co-dependent and Christian. Our individual relationship with God or spiritual direction by others can give us deep insights.

The second part is reading and study, both spiritual and recovery-oriented. This appeals to our intellectual side and helps us to see a perspective and overview concerning our goals and our ideals. It gives us information and a framework in which to make sense of the work that we have to do. It goes a long way in helping us to understand.

Part three is communication. This occurs on all different levels with friends, family, counselor, clergyperson, etc. We are able to give and receive valuable feedback and test our "reality wings," if you will. In this human interaction, valuable lessons are learned about myself, the people that I confide in, and the world in which I live.

The fourth part is counseling/therapy, if appropriate. If on my own or through my interaction with other people, reading material, or in prayer, I come to the decision to pursue a therapeutic relationship, whether formalized or non-formalized, this would certainly be advisable. The therapeutic process can be a valuable source of insight and self-knowledge that is a great asset in the journey of life.

Practicing new behaviors is a fifth suggestion. This is not meant in the sense of a cruise advertisement which suggests "being someone else" for a week because you'll never see these people again! Rather, for example, I mean trying to be more assertive with authority figures in your life, or doing nice things for yourself, or stop taking work home at night, or learning to say "No" with a smile instead of saying "Yes" with a grimace. These actions will help us put a stop to some of the vicious cycles of Christian co-dependency in our lives. These actions will result in changed feelings over time. And that's what we're trying to accomplish.

Last, but not least, is participation in self-help groups. This enables one to interact with several people at a time — people who have some semblance of commonality by virtue of the fact that they too are going to the meetings — in a relatively safe place, where the sense of not being alone is present, as well as, an educational environment for sharing feelings. The group may be Adult Children of Alcoholics [or Other Dysfunctional Families] (ACoA), Families Anonymous (FA), Codependents Anonymous (CoDA), or some other self-help group. As the name implies, the individual is helped through sharing experiences of others and with others. (For a list of the Twelve Steps of Recovery refer to Appendix V.)

WHEN does this happen? The only time for it is in the present. We have, for too long, felt guilt, regret and anger about the past. We spend far too much time worrying and being anxious about the future. But, as Mr. Keating told his pupils in *The Dead Poet's Society, Carpe Diem*! "Seize the Day!" Approach each day with zest and vitality! Think for yourself! Feel your feelings!

Today

The best thing you have in this world is today. Today is your savior; it is often crucified between two thieves, yesterday and tomorrow. Most of our misery is left over

It is noteworthy that in the Old Testament the manna that
was found in the desert was provided on a daily basis, but could
not be hoarded or stored from one day to the next. In the
Lord's Prayer, we are told to ask for our "daily bread." There
are also admonitions about needless worry: "Which of you
by worrying can add a moment to his life-span? If the smallest
things are beyond your power, why be anxious about the rest?"
(Luke 12:25-26) And, the wisdom of self-help groups focuses
on the present moment, saying to take it "One Day At a
Time."

Although Jesus asks us to repent, to convert (to "turn
toward"), and to undergo *metanoia*, a radical change of heart,
He cautions about dwelling in the past also: ". . . Whoever
puts his hand to the plow but keeps looking back is unfit for
the reign of God." (Luke 9:62)

This is how our life unfolds. It is a series of *today*'s that
are strung together. It seems to me that we're more willing
to accept starting over in athletics when a team or a player
has a "bad season," or in business when a company goes
bankrupt, than we are with our sense of sinfulness. We can
be our own worst enemies by succombing to the Evil One's
temptation and diminishing our own greatness and our role
in God's plan. We do this by dwelling on our guilt and sin
and responding to God's call with "I can't", "I won't!", "Not
me!", "Let George do it!"; with complacency and apathy.
Sometimes it seems like it's too late or "I'll never get out of

these habits!'' But we must remember that God chose the weak to confound the strong. It is never too late to start again, to be "born again" and I'm never too old to start again, because "Today is the first day of the rest of my life!"

Do we get to pick and choose WHERE this process will happen? "Yes" and "No." The most crucial decision is the decision even to start this process. Once that commitment has been made, we cannot "straddle the fence," so to speak. Because if we are not working on our recovery, we probably are sliding back into those old non-recovering, co-dependent Christian behaviors. Once we have been "found," that dynamic of being found becomes the driving force behind our actions and our thoughts. If we do start to separate or deny or isolate, and say "Well, I need to work on these issues at home, because that's where I have a real problem," but we ignore or deny the very same issues' existence in the workplace, then we are repeating the very same self-destructive behaviors that we set out to change. If, on the other hand, we only try to change our behavior at work, but do nothing to enhance our self-esteem and sense of identity with our friends, we are picking and choosing. Just as we are not called to be Christian in only certain situations, we cannot divide our heart and mind and soul in terms of our co-dependency recovery. This is one of those all or nothing affairs! I believe we are called to be recovering, co-dependent Christians in all aspects of our life — at work, at play, at home, at worship, in politics, and in society in general. If we're not, what good does it do? What difference does it make? We are a totality, a whole person, not a subdivided one. We cannot say, "OK, this spiritual part of me can recover, but my emotional part is off limits!"

This is not to say that it may take time for us to work up the courage and stamina to do certain things in this recovery process, like stick up for ourselves, set boundaries, confront abusive people in our lives, and take time for ourselves. But our overall attitude and direction needs to be re-Christianized and recovery oriented. Sometimes it may seem that for every step forward, we take two steps backward. This is to be expected. But every "today" gives us new challenges and opportunities to grow, to learn, and become. Like the stock market or growing older, the gradual movement is forward.

If there is still doubt about undertaking this process, let's discuss it. WHY bother with all of this?

In Chinese character writing, the word for "crisis" is made up of two characters, one meaning "danger," and the other, "opportunity." When I began my co-dependency recovery journey, and again when I began to feel this apparent conflict between my Christian faith and my recovery program, I felt that I was in a state of crisis. The danger was that I would merely continue to put a bandaid on a wound that needed major surgery, and that I would simply perpetuate the vicious cycle in which I found myself. In the past, after I got over the pain and the anger and the self-doubt, the defense mechanisms and denial returned in a few days or weeks. Then, I would be "back to normal" until it happened the next time. And I was getting tired and frustrated and angry about there even having to be a "next time" in this cycle.

The opportunity was centered in the fact that by some very difficult, very painful work, I could grow, learn and develop to the point of breaking this cycle of co-dependency and that I would be aided by my faith rather than being alienated from it. That I had the possibility of attaining freedom, self-esteem, and genuine love by discovering and being myself was an exciting opportunity! Although I have never given birth to a child, I am told that the joy, the sense of peace and mystery, and thankfulness afterwards make the pain worth it. To me, that's the case with this process as well.

I see this dynamic as one of the ways of individualizing the Paschal Mystery — the life, suffering and death, and resurrection of Jesus Christ. It is a dying to the "old" self — the self that is wracked with pain and conflict and lack of identity — and rising to the "new" self that is full of life, humanness, love and faith. Jesus said, "I solemnly assure you, unless the grain of wheat falls to the earth and dies, it remains just a grain of wheat. But if it dies, it produces much fruit. The man who loves his life loses it, while the man who hates his life *in this world* (italics added) preserves it to eternal life. If anyone would serve me, let him follow me; where I am, there will my servant be." (John 12:24-26) This is "Good News," but it is by no means "Easy News."

Another reason why a recovering co-dependent Christian, a found Christian, needs to be involved in this process is to break the vicious cycle of addiction. Addiction, after all, is fundamentally a spiritual issue. I see addiction as the process of wanting to escape this journey of self-discovery, of growth, of being in touch with my God-centeredness, of self-actualization — of being human and of being myself. The addict does not like himself or the world that he sees, so rather than working on himself and that world, he decides to create one of his own. He tries to run away, but as a child trying to lose his shadow, he can never run far enough or fast enough or long enough to succeed. He is stuck. I see addiction as a distraction and distortion that causes us to de-focus from feelings and our spirituality. Addiction is counter-productive, self-indulgent compulsion, whether it's centered on food, sex, drugs, work, worry, gambling, relationships, co-dependency, etc. It focuses on negativism and criticism. Viewed in this manner, many of us will qualify as "addicts."

Finally, as a Christian co-dependent, the only purpose of this journey of self-discovery and self-love is to more fully appreciate God's gift of myself and then to give this gift away — not to have power, wealth, influence, or the ability to judge others, but to serve, to love, to create the Kingdom, and to be a better instrument of God.

The co-dependent Christian's efforts to "do God's Will" have been a source of conflict in the past due to misunderstanding and misinterpretation. My belief is that when my relationships with myself, with others and with God are all in harmony, then I am doing God's Will. The graphic representation of this would be a circle, rather than a triangle or an elipse, where one or the other of these elements is out of kilter. I do not believe that one of these relationships can dominate or that one can be neglected to the detriment of the other(s).

(And for the lost, co-dependent Christian, the element that has suffered the most is the "self.") Remember, being the best "me" that I can be, for the Christian co-dependent, means being in a recovery process and truly loving myself; being the best "me" that I can be and being "all that I can be" means giving God the greatest glory; and being the best "me" and realizing my potential means being the most loving and best Christian witness in my relationships with others. It's both simple and profound how this has helped me to unify my life in terms of spiritual, personal, professional, relationship and everyday issues.

Gabriel Moran states that, "The adult has to be dependent in an independent way and independent in a dependent way."[19] And Melody Beattie uses Penelope Russianoff's term, "Undependence" to describe "that desirable balance wherein we acknowledge and meet our healthy, natural needs for people and love, yet we don't become overly or harmfully dependent on them."[20] With God's help, this is the co-dependent Christian's goal.

Now that we have seen some direction for the "found," recovering co-dependent Christian to take, let's look at this person in light of our ten Scriptural values.

Reflection/Discussion Questions

How have you tried to deal with this conflict in the past? How do the author's five steps provide direction?

How would you describe God's Will, in general? How would you describe God's Will for you?

Were you familiar with this human/emotional Jesus? Can you relate to Him? Were you taught this vision of Jesus?

Do you see a need for "Christian Recovery" in your life?

Are you ready, willing, and able to make some changes in your life?

How would you describe your relationship with yourself, with others, and with God?

Do you have a positive attitude toward yourself? If not, what would it take to become positive?

Do you need to counteract "old rules" from your past?

(Refer to Appendix V) Could a Twelve Step Program be helpful to you in this process? What actions can you take to help you feel better about yourself, your faith and your relationships?

Look at yourself and see what is right instead of what is wrong — make a list of *only* your good qualities and talents.

Name five things that give you pleasure and have no monetary cost. When was the last time you *did* each of them? What makes you feel "good" about yourself?

Where do you receive your support from? Name a caring, loving group that you belong to.

Recall a time when you felt (a) manipulated, and (b) assertive. What feelings did each situation create?

What basic requirements do you need for yourself before being able to care for others?

What creative outlets do you have? What can you do to foster more creativity in yourself?

Name a problem that you have encountered where you feel you did your best.

CHAPTER V
The Recovering Co-dependent Christian And The Ten Mandates

Let there be peace on earth and let it begin with me.[1]
(*This song speaks about peace spreading over the earth by each individual's commitment, in harmony with mankind, and in the unity of God. But, it begins with each "me."*)

In this song we see an individual's desire to have an impact, not only on herself, but ultimately on the world. Far fetched? Not really. In today's world that is constantly growing smaller by improvements in communications and technology, we see the effects of the inventors of fiber optics and the fax machine. We also have witnessed the peace initiatives of Bush and Gorbachev and their effects — arms reduction, greater religious and political freedom, the tearing down of the Berlin Wall. And we have seen the social effects of movements such as the Peace Corps and Habitat for Humanity. And let us not forget the thousands of saints and heroes who go about their daily lives performing miracles and doing God's work, such as Mother Teresa and Ralph Delaney, a Clevelander who worked with the poor in the projects who was killed one night by a group of thugs. Each of these actions was performed by an individual in conjunction with other individuals — by a "me" with a hope and a vision.

Using The Christopher's motto that "it is better to light one candle than to curse the darkness," we can see that by starting from within, as a recovering co-dependent Christian, we can make necessary changes in our own lives that will carry over into the lives of others. The peace and love within our own hearts can become contagious!

In this two-pronged process of being both Christian *and* a recovering co-dependent, the tension that exists is between the outward flow of Christianity and the inward ebb of recovery.

But, as we have seen, that tension is more superficial than the core of the concepts. Both Christianity and co-dependency recovery start with the self, with our individual consciousness and sense of reality. Both start small. In the Old Testament, there's a passage of God relating to Elijah that goes like this: "Then the Lord said, 'Go outside and stand on the mountain before the Lord; the Lord will be passing by.' A strong and heavy wind was rending the mountains and crushing rocks before the Lord — but the Lord was not in the wind. After the wind there was an earthquake — but the Lord was not in the earthquake. After the earthquake there was a fire — but the Lord was not in the fire. After the fire there was a tiny whispering sound. When he heard this, Elijah hid his face in his cloak and went and stood at the entrance of the cave." (1 Kings 19:11-13)

Two significant things stand out in this passage. First, the Lord was not found in the dramatic, powerful manifestations of nature but, rather, He made Himself known in a "tiny whispering sound." Secondly, when the Lord made Himself known, Elijah knew it! I think this is the case with each of us as well. That "tiny whispering sound" within each of us is the voice of the Lord calling us to follow Him, calling us to recovery, calling us to be ourselves. And when we hear it, we know it. Let's look at what this means in terms of our Scriptural mandates.

Faith. The gift of faith calls forth belief in God and in myself. It evokes the ultimate self-fulfilling prophecy — to live what I believe. In feeling better about myself I can now more easily accept what God has been telling me all along! I am God's child, I am worthwhile and lovable, and there is a unique place for me in the universe!

I can more easily turn my life over to God's care as I free myself of self-defeating and self-destructive behaviors. I can more vigorously respond to the call to discipleship when I come from a position of high self-esteem and self-love, rather than

one of woundedness, brokenness and victimization. And that's
what God wants for us! Everything's not going to be rosy.
We need to accept those challenges that we are given, whether
they are physical, mental, emotional, or matters of wealth or
talent. (To whom much is given, much is expected.) I believe
that one of life's greatest challenges is not only accepting the
cards that we are dealt, but also how we play our hand.

Jesus said, " 'I assure you, if you had faith the size of a
mustard seed, you would be able to say to this mountain,
'Move from here to there,' and it would move. Nothing would
be impossible for you.' " (Matthew 17:20) Surely, our faith
is greater than the size of a mustard seed! And if it's really
true that the greater our faith, the greater our ability to give
glory to God by being His instruments and by being ourselves,
then, the sky is the limit!

Our hound Ziggy is ten years old. There's a proverb that
says "You can't teach an old dog new tricks." Well, just in
these last few weeks we have in fact taught her a new trick.
She now knows how to carry a plastic plate with a biscuit taped
to it from me to my wife. Marge then gives her the biscuit and
Ziggy returns the plate very proudly to me. So much for
proverbs! But my point is, had we believed the proverb, we
never would have even *thought* about trying to teach something else to Ziggy at her age. How much more important is
this concept in terms of our own lives and our vision! If we
believe that we can't change, that we are helpless in this struggle
with co-dependency, and that our life can't get better, the self-
fulfilling prophecy will work — we will not change, we will
continue to feel helpless and our lives will not get better!

Father John Powell, S. J., talks about his thoughts about
the Apostles: "Once I thought that the Twelve Apostles were
a bit slow, that they were missing the candlepower or intelligence to learn the lessons of their Master. I had counted seven-
teen places in the Gospels where Jesus asks them, 'Are you
yet without understanding?' In our present-day jargon, we
would probably translate this, 'You don't get it yet, do you?'
I once thought these things, but not now. I now think that

the real challenge of Jesus was not a matter of intelligence, but ultimately a challenge to give up an old vision and to accept a new one. It was a matter of radical faith and profound trust."[2]

Through this recovery process of self-love and re-examining our Christian heritage, I feel there is a radical new vision that is made known to the co-dependent Christian, the "found" Christian. That vision is that truly being myself and loving myself and truly loving others and being a follower of Christ are all in harmony. We are asked to try to live that vision in our everyday lives, trusting and believing that God is with us on this journey. It's sort of like the Ohio Lottery ad that says, "You can't win if you don't play!" — we have to take that risk and believe, to take that leap of faith.

Jesus calls for us to believe with our strongest faith.

Truth. With our new vision of faith, we "found" Christians are now better equipped to accept the Truth — the Truth about Jesus Christ, the Truth about ourselves and the Truth about other people and our interaction with them. Jesus Christ, as the Truth, has set us free from Sin as well as from our old mind-sets and ways of thinking and acting. As Father John Powell, S. J. calls it, Jesus challenges us to "stretch." Jesus asks us to leap forward but also to accept our imperfection and our weakness, in true humility. We are weak, but we are strong. We are flesh, but we are spirit. We are sinners, but we are saved. Our life takes place neither in black nor white, but mostly in the balance of gray that's in between. Often, we settle for so little compared to what we can really be or become.

Part of the "stretching" process is to see God in a different light, such as Mother God, and, perhaps unlike our parents, as One who loves us unconditionally. Part of it is to see ourselves through different eyes, the eyes of love and recovery, and affirmation and acceptance. And part of it is to see other people with a different vision, a vision of independence and self-sufficiency — that they don't need us to take care of them. We don't have to compete, either. We don't have to tear the other person down in order for us to feel better, nor do we have to tear ourselves down for the other person to feel better. Another aspect of that vision is that we don't need to manipulate others to achieve salvation, theirs or ours!

We can face our fears with greater confidence: our fear of love, of intimacy, of ourselves, of others, of God and of trusting. We can replace doubt with possibility; rigidity, with openness; and control, with spontaneity. We can trust the process of co-dependency recovery, knowing that the more we practice these principles, the better we will feel.

The truth of the matter is that it's OK to be me! And this pilgrimage takes a lifetime. It's not a contest or a race. Father Joseph Gallagher states that "our summons is to set each other free."[3] But this marvel does not happen overnight. Jesus recognized the limitations of our human hearts and minds, and He left continuing revelation to the Spirit: "I have much more to tell you, but you cannot bear it now. When he comes, however, being the Spirit of truth he will guide you to all truth." (John 16:12-13)

We have this cat, Duffy, who has been a boarder at our house for eight years now. He was a wild, starving kitten when we found him in the backyard. He was so happy that he purred almost non-stop for the first two days, even while getting a bath! But then he noticed how big and loud Ziggy is and he has been afraid of us since then. Somehow he associates us with the dog, the source of his fear. We literally have to catch him in order to pet him. Basically he hides and runs from us except at feeding time. Duffy will purr when we catch him, but otherwise he is not a pet or a domestic cat, nor is he wild — he could not survive just by his instincts. He's an animal spirit trapped in a cat's body. His only friend is our other cat. He doesn't know the joy of sleeping on someone's lap or playing with a toy tossed by a person — things that a cat is supposed to do. He is dominated by fear, both of us and of Ziggy. It's sad, but Duffy doesn't know who he's supposed to be. We are sometimes in that painful place, but the Truth can set us free! Our mandate is to become ourselves!

It is also true that some of these personality traits that are characteristic of co-dependency are also our assets as well. Responsibility, dedication, compassion, concern, thoughtfulness, eagerness, volunteerism, etc. are all desirable traits when considered in balance and when they do not boomerang and harm us.

Just as God's Will involves my having a good relationship with myself, with others and with God, so too, "being myself" involves this same triad. Because I am "person," I need to be at peace with myself. Because I am "social," I need to be in relationship to other humans. Because I am "spiritual," I need to be in touch with God. Because I am Christian, I need to be all three. This also is Truth.

Jesus asks us for our most noble truth.

Love. This is a Scriptural definition of God as well as the commandment of Jesus. It is a tall order to live up to. You have to experience it in order to believe it and to have a vague idea of what it is. Songs talk about it all the time, and we use it to describe how we feel about everything from pizza to Pontiacs. But, with our new recovery-oriented understanding and our re-Christianized view of love, we are less prone to accept counterfeits. And we are more likely to give some to ourselves.

We also need to realize that being in harmony with others does not mean that everything is "hunky dory" with absolutely everyone else. There are people that we need to be at odds with, because they are abusive, doing evil, or trying to drag us down with them. Although Jesus told us to love our enemies, according to John, the greatest love is to lay down your life for your friends.

There's a saying that, "Charity begins at home." It originally meant that love and kindness should start in one's family, rather than neglecting those closest to us, while showing charity to outsiders. Well, in this recovery process, charity begins with us as well, rather than with others. Then there's another saying that the best thing that parents can do for their children is for the parents to love each other. The children will absorb this love and be imbued with it, so that they too will feel it. The same principle applies to the "found," recovering co-dependent Christian: the best thing we can do for *others* is to love *ourselves*, because that true love then naturally flows outward to others. It can't be bottled up or contained. We are called to love ourselves unconditionally, with one eye on the fact that there is always room for improvement, but the other, on the fact that I am worthy of love, not because of what I do, but because of who I am. A bird sings, not because it has a reason, but because it has a song.

Melody Beattie in *Co-dependent No More* quotes Nathaniel Branden in his book, *Honoring the Self*:

> " 'To honor the self is to be in love with our own life, in love with our possibilities for growth and for experiencing joy, in love with the process of discovery and exploring our distinctively human potentialities.
>
> Thus we can begin to see that to honor the self is to practice selfishness *in the highest, noblest, and least understood sense of that word. And this, I shall argue, requires enormous independence, courage, and integrity.'*
>
> We need to love ourselves and make a commitment to ourselves. We need to give ourselves some of the boundless loyalty that so many codependents are willing to give others. Out of high self-esteem will come true acts of kindness and charity, not selfishess.
>
> The love we give and receive will be enhanced by the love we give ourselves.'"[4]

By knowing and loving myself, I am able to be a more effective instrument of God. I can see counterfeits of love as just that, counterfeits. I can embrace intimacy — teaching you about me and vice versa — with greater confidence, because I am more certain of who I am and because I feel good about myself. I can love more genuinely by letting you be you and allowing me to be me. I don't have to control and manipulate and be someone I'm not.

In his first letter, John writes, "We for our part, love because he first loved us. If anyone says, 'My love is fixed on God,' yet hates his brother, he is a liar. One who has no love for the brother he has seen cannot love the God he has not seen. The commandment we have from him is this: whoever loves God must also love his brother." (1 John 5:19-21) And the triad is completed by Jesus — whoever loves his neighbor must also love himself! Jesus could have said to us, "Love yourself as much as you love your neighbor." Rejoice! We have God's blessing to recover!

Jesus calls for our deepest, most genuine love.

Free Will. Choice. Decision. Freedom. These are words in God's vocabulary. God does not want us to be robots, or zombies, or puppets. He does not want us to say a blind "yes" to anyone who approaches us! Let's face it, many people do in fact seem to choose evil! Look at Hitler, Jim Jones, Jeffery Lundgren and other mind-control artists. God wants us to be whole, healthy, instruments and witnesses — ourselves. I believe that He is against whatever it is that keeps us from doing that. He does not want us always being a sucker and compromising our values and principles just because someone had the nerve to ask us to do something and we're afraid to say, "No." Where do we draw the line? We have to discern and utilize our free will and to set boundaries.

And that is why it is so important to include being in harmony with myself as one facet of doing God's Will. I have to trust my feelings and believe in myself — if it doesn't feel right to me, then I need to step back and question and examine the situation, rather than just blindly following along. Obedience has its place, but it also depends on the circumstances.

Jesus said, ". . . If a man wishes to come after me, he must deny his very self, take up his cross, and begin to follow in my footsteps. Whoever would save his life will lose it, but whoever loses his life for my sake will find it. What profit would a man show if he were to gain the whole world and destroy himself in the process? What can a man offer in exchange for his very self?'' (Matthew 16:24-26) Jesus lays it on the line! He's giving an invitation to a friend, not a command to a subject. We do have a choice. And, He's talking about the self and one's own life, not the other guy's.

Decisions are difficult enough for a co-dependent person to make. But in this Christian recovery process, I can more easily make the decision to take care of myself as well as to reaffirm my decision to follow Jesus Christ. By knowing myself better and truly loving myself, by my free choice, I am able to truly sacrifice, not just be caught up in an abusive or manipulative situation, and call it sacrifice, dedication, and love. God does not want us to respond by accident or out of duty or obligation. He wants our freely given love, not our coerced contempt.

In my recovery process, as I feel better about myself, my need to have high expectations of others, who in the past provided the major reflection of my self-image, is not as great, and therefore I have more freedom to be me and to let the other be the other.

But we must remember that another aspect of our connectedness is doing God's Will. In my freedom, as a Christian, I choose to allow God to work in me and through me. By virtue of that decision I am entering a partnership with God — I am letting go and letting God. There is no longer a dictatorship in my life, whether that dictator was me, God or other people.

Jesus wants our most soaring, magnificent freedom.

Responsibility. With this new perspective of the ''found'' Christian, I have a better sense of responsibility. I can set limits and boundaries without feeling guilty. I can appreciate the fact that being overly responsible, to the point of controlling and manipulating, is as counterproductive as being irresponsible. My responsibility is limited. Although it is primary in my own life, it is not ultimate or divine. That's God's job. (This partnership that I'm in with God, is a limited partnership, Ltd.) My faith is a gift to me alone and it does not depend on some*thing* or some*one* else. My faith relationship with God is self-actualizing, and circular, therefore involving others as well.

There's a saying that goes, "If you give someone a fish, he has food for today; if you teach him how to fish, he has food for a lifetime." In our new vision, we don't have to *do* for someone or *give* them something merely because it's easier for us or more convenient or makes us look good. Like giving them a fish. We can make a commitment and enter into a relationship with someone, like teaching them how to fish, but obviously we are limited in our abilities in this regard. We do not have to over-extend ourselves to everyone, nor are we capable of doing this. We can't possibly teach everyone to fish! Only God can be all things to all people. (Plus, He knows where the fish are!)

But that, again, is where our responsibility comes in. We have to make choices as to whom our time, effort, and support will be given. We are called upon continuously to make choices, and that can feel burdensome. But it also keeps us active, "on our toes," involved with our brothers and sisters, and alive!

In this regard, loving, serving and helping my neighbor is not automatically a co-dependent behavior that goes against my recovery process. Rather, it is my free choice of being God's instrument and putting into motion that circular pattern of God's Will — striving for harmony with myself, my neighbor and my God. Because, when I say "yes" to Jesus, it is an all or none proposition. I cannot have a "salad bar" mentality, whereby I pick what I like and what I'm used to, but ignore what might be difficult, or painful or uncomfortable in the Gospel. In saying that "yes," I am a totality, a whole person, and I'm making a commitment for richer, for poorer; in sickness and in health; for easy and for difficult; for known and for unknown.

I must follow the dictates of my conscience, and through prayer and discernment, I must respond, in the ways that I am able, to God's call. And this is intrinsically involved in that growth process of becoming myself.

Jesus wants our wisest, most creative response to Him.

Healing And Forgiveness. Like love, this is a two-edged sword. We are called to be instruments of healing and forgiveness, both to ourselves and to others. Perhaps the biggest news is that we can now do this to and for ourselves first. We can more readily allow God to forgive and heal us, as well. This then has all kinds of ramifications for our relationships with other people. Since I no longer need to be so critical of and hard on myself, I find that mercy and compassion become easier to express and to receive.

Just as with the adulteress, when Jesus asked for those who were without sin to cast the first stone (John 8:7), we now know that we do not have to cast the first stone at ourselves!

Jesus asks us to be as open and receptive to the healing aspect (which occurs on spiritual, emotional, psychological and physical planes) as we are to the forgiveness aspect, which we usually associate with the forgiveness of sins. After all, it was Jesus who brought up the relationship between healing and the forgiveness of sins: "When Jesus saw their faith, he said to the paralyzed man, 'My son, your sins are forgiven.' Now some of the scribes were sitting there asking themselves: 'Why does the man talk in that way? He commits blasphemy! Who can forgive sins except God alone?' Jesus was immediately aware of their reasoning, though they kept it to themselves, and he said to them: 'Why do you harbor these thoughts? Which is easier, to say to the paralytic, 'Your sins are forgiven,' or to say, 'Stand up, pick up your mat, and walk again?' That you may know that the Son of Man has authority on earth to forgive sins' (he said to the paralyzed man), 'I command you: Stand up! Pick up your mat and go home.' The man stood and picked up his mat and went outside in the sight of everyone. They were awestruck; all gave praise to God, saying, 'We have never seen anything like this!' " (Mark 2:5-12)

It was also Jesus who noted the relationship between love and forgiveness: "Turning then to the woman, he said to Simon: 'You see this woman? I came to your home and you provided me with no water for my feet. She has washed my feet with her tears and wiped them with her hair. You gave me no kiss, but she has not ceased kissing my feet since I entered. You did not anoint my head with oil, but she has anointed my feet with perfume. I tell you, that is why her many sins are forgiven — because of her great love. Little is forgiven the one whose love is small.' '' (Luke 7:44-50)

As recovering co-dependents, we are in need of healing the pain, guilt and shame that we feel. We are also in need of healing our memories and our feelings. We are in need of healing that child within us. We are in need of forgiveness of our sins and the wrongs that we have done. We are in need of God's forgiveness, our own forgiveness and that of others. We are in need of healing of mind, body and soul.

But we are also God's instruments of healing and forgiveness to ourselves and others as well. (After experiencing healing and forgiveness, we are then able to share it with others.) God's mercy is ever-present. It is a bottomless well, waiting to be tapped. All we need to do is muster the courage, love and humility to ask. Jesus said, ''So I say to you, 'Ask and you shall receive; seek and you shall find; knock and it shall be opened to you. For whoever asks, receives; whoever seeks, finds; whoever knocks is admitted.' '' (Luke 11:9-10)

Jesus asks for our most merciful healing and forgiveness.

Suffering And Death. As Christians, we have always known that Jesus conquered sin and set us free from the finality of death by His own passion and death. Now we know — through the recovery process that we have examined — that He has also set us free from ourselves! At times we are our own worst enemies, a la Pogo, ''We have met the enemy and he is us!'' In this problem of being a co-dependent Christian, we have been confused, mislead, misunderstood, and in pain. At times the ''Good News'' has felt like a millstone around our necks because it seemed to be tearing us down and eating us up inside!

But no more! By coming to know myself better, by taking time for myself, by loving myself — by becoming aware of my own identity — I can make true sacrifices of denying that self. Jesus who loved us so much would not ask us to do something that would harm or degrade us.

Sacrifice out of frustration and despair is not complete. By offering up my life out of strength rather than weakness, I can participate in the dying to self that Jesus spoke about. This, then, becomes a way of fulfilling myself as a Christian, as a person. Throughout history, God asked for the sacrifice of the best (the fatted calf, for example) and the first-born, not the runts or the weaklings. (Yet He used the weak and the small and the poor to confound the strong and the mighty and the wealthy, just showing the mysterious ways of God.)

Death comes for all of us in its own time. And Suffering is often Death's traveling companion. Although Death is the doorway to eternal life, Suffering is often the hall leading to that doorway. We don't have to seek suffering, but we are given an opportunity to accept it. It's part of how we play the hand that we are dealt. It comes with being human.

We can help to sanctify our suffering by offering it back to God — by using it as an opportunity — in our daily struggles for growth, recovery, discovery and in living our humanity. It is part of the process of accepting the fact that I am not God, and that suffering and death are part of the human condition. As much as we would like to believe otherwise, we are finite. The hour of our birth is the beginning of our march to the hour of our death. And God sets the heavenly timer until we are "done" on earth and are called to return home.

The word "compassion" means to "suffer together." We no longer have to suffer *for* someone or *instead* of someone. We can just *be* with them. We don't have to "fix" them or gloss over their pain or their feelings, or our own, for that matter. We can also ask for help when we are in need of aid and compassion.

Jesus literally "hung in there" from His place on the cross and He asks us to imitate Him. After the Resurrection, when talking to Peter, Jesus said: "I tell you solemnly: as a young man you fastened your belt and went about as you pleased; but when you are older you will stretch out your hands, and another will tie you fast and carry you off against your will.' (What he said indicated the sort of death by which Peter was to glorify God.) When Jesus had finished speaking he said to him, 'Follow me.' '' (John 21:18-19)

And in another place, Jesus said: '' 'This is my commandment: love one another as I have loved you. There is no greater love than this: to lay down one's life for one's friends.' '' (John 15:12-13)

This is the cost of discipleship. But we no longer need to fear death. Death will still be an unknown till we experience it. But *we* will no longer be an unknown quantity, someone to be feared. Our self-knowledge, self-love, and self-understanding — being ourselves — will enable us to approach the doorway of Death with greater confidence and faith than we ever thought possible. And our God will also become better known so we have less to fear.

Jesus wants our most courageous suffering and death.

Resurrection. Suffering and death are the means to an end. We are redeemed. We are saved. We can change. We are free to be that which God intended, ourselves. In the Resurrection, Jesus conquered the ultimate barriers, Sin and Death. The Resurrection is the Ultimate Possibility. We are no longer doomed to the quicksand of Sin, but we can rise to the glory of salvation as did Peter, Mary Magdalene, Paul, Augustine, and countless others through the ages. Conversion, turning our hearts toward God, makes all the difference.

Through our death to our ''old self,'' we can accept the challenge of co-dependency recovery to be ''born again.'' We can change, we are capable, we are worthy. We can grow and strive to be our best selves. We can tear down walls and barriers and fears that bind and limit us. We no longer have to give lip service to being saved and being Christian, but we can truly believe it!

We are free of the shackles of co-dependency! We are free of the old ''wineskins'' that we inherited from those who taught us our Christian values but were unaware of the pitfalls of co-dependency and self-defeating behaviors. We are free to follow Jesus in a more personal, self-fulfilling way. We are free to make better choices. We are free to try. We are free to succeed. We are free of our past. We are only limited by the narrowness of our vision.

The Resurrection allows us to transcend our encumbered selves. It makes contact with the Spirit of God within us. It allows caterpillars to become butterflies. It allows co-dependent Christians to grow, change and get well.

Jesus proclaims our most glorious, transforming participation in His Resurrection.

Grace. Father John Powell, S. J. says grace is like being plugged into God's electrical current. To carry the analogy a bit further, when we are open to God's grace, we are like the "hot" wire in the circuit. We are the actors, the energy producers, the instruments of God on earth. The other wire, the wire that completes the circuit, is other people, those to whom we are intertwined in this life. The "ground" of the entire proces is the "contact with the earth," God. He is also our contact with the Spirit. Together this combination keeps the current flowing, keeps us in contact, keeps us "connected."

As recovering, co-dependent Christians, we are better able to accept the daily challenges of life and respect our individual role in God's plan. We can look for the opportunities that are present in our daily lives, not in a Pollyanna sort of way, but in a daily struggle sort of way. Scott Peck in *The Road Less Traveled* defines grace as "a powerful force originating outside human consciousness which nurtures the spiritual growth of human beings."[5] He goes on to say that, "The paradox that we both choose grace and are chosen by grace is the essence of the phenomenon of serendipity." [He defines serendipity as "the gift of finding valuable or agreeable things not sought for."][6]

But I am convinced that we have to know where to look. Since my wife and I bought the house we currently live in, which is on the edge of a thousand-acre park and has a small creek running next to it, we have become bird watchers. It has been a pleasure to learn about, observe and discover the wonders of nature present in birds and other wild animals. Through practice, education, trial and error, and just plain experience, she and I have become much more attuned to the sights and sounds of the bird world. We are much less oblivious to the hints and cues that many people ignore even in their own backyards! We have learned where to look and what to look for.

So, too, with serendipity and with God's grace. Through our recovery process and being more positive and loving with ourselves, we can more clearly see the Hand of God in our own lives through those people and events that have either crossed our paths or joined us on the journey. This is really exciting to take note of God's continuing revelation in and through our own lives! And part of that revelation is our own call to this recovery process. As Paul states in his letter to the Romans, "If God is for us, who can be against us?" (Romans 8:31)

Jesus calls for our greatest reliance on and use of God's grace.

Mystery And Paradox. We cannot really remove the mystery and paradox from the Christian message or from the co-dependency recovery process. The mystery and paradox are inherent in both. As recovering co-dependent Christians — as "found" Christians — we are better equipped to accept the seeming contradictions, the unexplainable, the mysterious aspects of our lives and what it means to be human as well as what it means to be a believer in Jesus Christ. We are better able to accept the mystery of opposites.

There are two facets to this issue. The one, as stated by Melody Beattie in *Co-dependent No More*, is that "Acceptance is the ultimate paradox: we cannot change who we are until we accept ourselves the way we are."[7] That is the beginning of the co-dependency recovery process as well as the starting point of our Christian faith. As the song at the beginning of this chapter states, "Let there be peace on earth and let it begin with me." (This is reminiscent of our questions in Chapter IV: WHO, me? WHAT can I do? WHEN can I possibly do this? WHERE can I make an impact? WHY should I bother?)

The second facet is the fact that recovery and fulfillment as a Christian are both possible and necessary for our "lost" Christian to be "found." As we have seen throughout this discussion, being a Christian and being involved in a co-dependency recovery process have the same goal — being the best *me* that I can be.

Sometimes the message of Jesus has those "hard sayings" and aspects that seem to be contradictory and divisive. In Scripture, we see that God is "all things to all people." He speaks to the proud and to the lowly; He speaks to the poor and to the rich; He speaks to the sick and to the healthy; He calls the holy and the worldly. That is why we need to continue to ask questions, to take a self inventory and not be judgmental, and to practice selfcare.

As recovering, co-dependent Christians, we are better able to accept the fact that many things in life are not bound by the rules of logic. Take love, for example. We say that love is "blind," or we say "I wonder what so-and-so sees in him/her?" So-and-so sees the beauty, the possibility, the Spirit in the other person. Jesus told us to love our enemies; He also said that in order to save our life we must first lose it. Twelve Step recovery programs tell us that we must first declare our powerlessness over our addiction or problem in order to attain some semblance of power and control over it. For some strange reason, it's only in surrendering that we can hope to win the battle! (I'm sure that this is never taught at military academies!)

Some other examples are rubbing compound, Ritalin and fire. How is it that in order to get a dull surface shiny and bright, you use a gritty abrasive like rubbing compound instead of a smooth polish? How is it that "speed," such as Ritalin, which makes "normal" people hyper and "wired," is used to calm down hyperactive children? And how is it that sometimes instead of using water to douse a fire, you have to start a fire in order to take the fuel away from the fire that you're trying to contain?

Throughout salvation history, God has worked miracles and surprised humankind. God said, "And all the trees of the field shall know that I, the Lord, bring low the high tree, lift high the lowly tree, wither up the green tree, and make the withered tree bloom. As I, the Lord, have spoken, so will I do." (Ezekiel 17:24) Elizabeth, who had been infertile, has a child in her old age. Jesus tells us that the last shall be first, and the first shall be last.

Many times God's ways are not our ways, and God's timetable is not ours. But part of the mystery is that we are, in fact, capable of this growth process as well as the promises of Jesus Christ's message. Jesus said, "The man who has faith in me will do the works I do, and greater far than these." (John 14:12) In our wildest dreams we cannot imagine what potential we have when we surrender to this recovery/growth process and embrace our re-discovered Christian faith!

Our lost treasure is under our noses. It is ourselves! This is not meant in an egotistical way but in true humility — being what we are and doing what we can AND thanking God because everything we are is His gift. Having embarked on this recovery process, combined with our faith commitment, and with love of God and love of others, we are strengthened to have a productive, wholesome, holy life.

Reflection/Discussion Questions

Can you visualize yourself with these positive, healthy attitudes? Will this attitude aid or hinder your Christian lifestyle?

(Refer to Appendix IV) Can you be assertive without being aggressive? Give some examples.

Which mandates do you need to work on? Which is your most difficult? Which is your easiest?

In what situations are you non-assertive? Assertive? Aggressive?

Recount a successful overcoming of a habit or behavior that you considered "bad."

Think of something very positive in your life and then think of something negative. Now visualize changing the negative thing into a positive thing.

What ways do you care for yourself?

Think of some unresolved conflict in your life and then visualize settling that conflict.

Conclusion

Amazing Grace

Amazing Grace! How sweet the sound
that saved a wretch like me!
I once was lost, but now am found,
was blind but now I see.

'Twas grace that taught my heart to fear,
and grace my fears relieved;
How precious did that grace appear
the hour I first believed!

Through many dangers, toils, and snares
I have already come;
'Tis grace has brought me safe thus far,
and grace will lead me home.

The Lord has promised good to me,
His word my hope secures;
He will my shield and portion be
as long as life endures.

When we've been there ten thousand years,
bright shining as the sun,
We've no less days to sing God's praise
than when we first begun.[1]

In our day and age when materialism is so rampant and in which advertisers try to mould our identity by the clothes we wear, the cars we drive, the beverages we drink, and the scents we use, it is often a struggle to just BE. In this time of quick solutions (e.g., by taking a pill to feel better), and quick resolution of a problem in a two hour movie, we become impatient with ourselves when the "quick fix" doesn't work or it takes too long. But as Father John Powell, S. J. states, "Growth is always a gradual process, a bridge slowly crossed and not a corner sharply turned."[2] And as we have seen throughout this discussion, we're not looking at a mere facade or marketing stereotype, but rather at our true self and identity — **BEING ME!** And it takes commitment to a long, often difficult journey.

Jesus didn't stay on the cross, He didn't stay in the tomb, He didn't stay on earth (in bodily form)! His life was one of change and process. (More and more, it seems as though change is the *only* constant.) As our role model, He is showing us the way. Rather than focusing on a fixed end point, we need to adapt to a fluid view of the process.

The Station

Tucked away in our subconscious is an idyllic vision. We see ourselves on a long trip that spans the continent. We are traveling by train. Out the windows we drink in the passing scene of cars on near-by highways, of children waving at a crossing.

But uppermost in our minds is the final destination. On a certain day, at a certain hour, we will pull into the station. Bands will be playing and flags waving. Once we get there, so many wonderful dreams will come true and the pieces of our lives will fit together like a completed jig-saw puzzle.

"When we reach the station, that will be it!" We cry. "When I'm 18." "When I put the last kid through college." "When I have paid off the mortgage."

Sooner or later we must realize there is no station, no one place to arrive at once and for all. The true joy of life is the trip. The station is only a dream.

"Relish the moment" is a good motto, especially when coupled with Psalm 118:24: "This is the day which the Lord hath made; we will rejoice and be glad in it." It isn't the burdens of today that drive men mad. It is the regrets over yesterday and the fear of tomorrow. Regret and fear are twin thieves who rob us of today.

So, stop pacing the aisles and counting the miles. Instead, climb more mountains, eat more ice cream, go barefoot more often, swim more rivers, watch more

And so it is in this lifelong effort of co-dependency recovery for a Christian person. It is not something that we must "get done with" or "get out of the way." Rather it becomes our way of living a Christian life. Through that truly "amazing grace" we who were lost are now found because we have been shown a way to truly love ourselves as well as our neighbors. We can visualize ourselves from the one end of God's continuum as being a mere speck in the universe — a mass of molecules and genetic material in the vast expanse of space and time — to the other end of that continuum where each of us is honored as an image of God Himself with a unique opportunity to be His instrument on this earthly sojourn and play our part in the Divine Agenda.

Only *I* can be myself and no one else can tell me who *I* am. No one else can take that self-ness from me. Hostages and captives have proven that over the centuries. Being myself is something that only God and I are privy to. Certainly people with whom I become friends and those others with whom I interact (and the way I interact with them) say something about who I am. But they do not define me. Every person I have met, every event in which I have participated, every word that I have spoken — whether truth or untruth — every experience that I have had, has "left its mark on me." My task is to digest, integrate and bring to awareness as much of this experience as possible so I can use it as a springboard to further my growth and development, my becoming. As our teachers have told us for years, the purpose in giving a test is not to find out what the student knows, but rather what the student does not know so that can be studied and learned in the future.

In the past, when we were "lost," we were lacking in understanding, confidence, awareness, recovery tools, and mature spiritual beliefs. But now that we are "found," we have a new perspective and a new vision. Like some desert plants whose seeds lay dormant for years until fertile rains cause them to sprout, and like the seeds of the "smoke bush" that lie in wait, possibly for decades, for a brush fire to pop them open so they can grow, the time has come! Like the Phoenix, a bird from ancient mythology, that rises triumphantly out of the ashes of its burnt nest, we who thought that our plight was hopeless, find that our lives can be full of hope! And again, this is possible at any age, any time, any place and any how.

This is by no means escapism or isolationism. As we become more comfortable with ourselves, and as our inward focus comes into balance with our outward focus — as it must — we are brought into the everyday "stuff" of life such as social issues, the environment, and the general well-being of our fellow men and women. We have come full circle, from low self-esteem and shame to a sense of true humility, high self-esteem and self-care. By then unlocking those positive personality traits that were out of control (such as responsibility, dedication, compassion, concern, thoughtfulness, eagerness, volunteerism, etc.), we find ourselves, once again, struggling to live the Gospel message and to help bring the Kingdom to earth. But the big difference is that this time we are being more open, more fair, and more loving, especially with ourselves.

So much for the "big picture." Each of us must acknowledge the Hand of God in our own, seemingly trivial, daily lives — to look at the "little picture" — as well. My guess is that when each of us looks back on our lives through the eyes of faith, and looks below the mere appearance of events and happenings, we find more than fate, coincidence, or luck —wehther we consider it to be good or bad. What we find, I believe, is the dynamic of grace, that we both choose and are chosen by, and serendipity (the gift of finding valuable or agreeable things not sought for) as explained by Scott Peck. My own history has several examples of this occuring.

The summer after I graduated from high school I didn't have much money saved to start college and my first year in the seminary in the Fall. My mother bought chances at our church festival for the five of us kids. She bought two for each of my brothers and my sister because they were all married and had bills, etc. She bought one chance for me. My ticket was something like 52,348 and even more than that were sold. I won! The prize was a thousand dollar savings bond which went a long way in helping me financially that year.

On New Year's Day 1976, Marge, three of my stepdaughters and I were driving to Chicago from Cleveland. It was a crisp, cold, sunny morning with dry roads on the Ohio Turnpike. Everyone was wearing a seatbelt and the others were sleeping or dozing off. I'm still not exactly sure what happened. Our 1972 VW bus had a floor shift. My travel case was on the floor near it. For some reason that bothered me. I leaned down to move it, and apparently pulled on the steering wheel. When I looked up, the car was going over a twelve- to fifteen-foot deep embankment that was on about a forty five degree angle. I panicked and tried to steer back up the grade, the wheels locked in the mud, and we rolled over two and a half times at fifty-five miles per hour (and no skid marks!). We came to rest on the driver's side and climbed out where the front windshield had been. Other than a few cuts and scratches, we were all OK! There was no fire, but the car was a total loss.

At the City of Cleveland/*Cleveland Press* New Year's Eve Party 1977 we won a car! We were not there, but I'm assuming the drawing was held around midnight. We were notified New Year's Day 1977, a year to the day after the accident!

In 1983 at the age of thirty-four I had a heart attack. As the youngest of four boys in a family with a predisposition to heart disease, I thought I was the safest. I appeared to be in the best shape — active lifestyle, not overweight, non-smoker, no high blood pressure. But because of stress, workaholism and a permanent genetic malfunction of my cholesterol filtration system, I was the first to have a heart attack! Why me? Because if I had not had a warning then that I needed to make changes in my lifestyle, I'm convinced that I would be dead by now without having made those changes. Despite my three-vessel cornary artery disease (or maybe because of it) God had other plans for me!

I tried hard to take care of myself that next year, and my weakened stamina plus the side effects of the medications that I was on also slowed me down. I couldn't have kept up my previous frantic pace even if I had wanted to.

Prior to my heart attack, I had been introduced to a healing ministry of a Catholic laywoman named Barbara O'Malley. The first time I went to the healing service I found it to be a very cathartic experience. I cried for about a half hour and I didn't know why. The next time I went was in the Spring of 1984. When Barbara went to pray over me, I told her about my heart condition and she put her hand on my chest as she prayed. I was praying for emotional, physical, psychological and spiritual healing. Although I was "slain in the Spirit," that is, fell backward into a restful state of peace, still conscious, and caught by someone to help lay me on the church floor, I did not feel anything in particular. I was tired after being at church for four hours, so I went home. Then Marge got a ride home. Later she told me that Barbara had said that someone was being healed of a heart condition and that no one there had "claimed" it. I did not think much of it.

The next morning was a beautiful, sunny, warm May morning. The grass was high because my riding mower had broken earlier that week and I had been cutting the grass with a gas hand mower. Earlier that week I could cut only for about 15-20 minutes and then I would have to rest. The day after the healing service I cut grass for an hour and fifteen minutes straight! I had worked up a sweat and lost track of time. I came in the house and sat down with Marge. I told her what happened. That day I did more physical work than on any day in the year since my heart attack.

A miracle? A healing? I think so. And that sense of healing has stayed with me ever since. I didn't throw away my medication, but my level of activity improved as well as my sense of spiritual, emotional and psychological well being.

On Ash Wednesday 1986, I had a second heart catherization. It showed that my 50 percent blockage and the 75 percent blockage had stayed the same. But the 90 percent blockage was now totally obstructed. However, I had developed collateral circulation. That is, two shoots, like the roots of a plant, had come out on each side of that artery above the obstruction, and joined the same artery below the blockage. Although they were small, they were large enough to appear on the angiogram. It amounted to a "natural bypass." It most likely was the cause of my increased circulation and stamina. It was also a sign of my physical healing. My cardiologist said that this phenomenon was not totally unheard of, but he also said it did not "happen everyday."

And, by the way, would you be surprised to hear that the date of that healing service, May 19, 1984, was a year to the day after my heart attack?!

A bit of serendipity occured in 1986 when someone at work put a little snippet of a classified ad in my mailbox. The ad concerned a chemical dependency counseling position with an agency in a neighboring county. I pursued it and got a contract position which began my part-time counseling career. But more importantly it led to my meeting my friend Joe who has had a very great impact on me in terms of my recovery process as well as my writing career. He first introduced me to the characteristics list of Adult Children of Alcoholics. We have spent many hours discussing recovery dynamics and supporting each others' writing endeavors, and becoming friends. Although I tried to pursue it, to this day, I have no idea who put that tiny ad in my mailbox.

In the Fall of 1987 I received CPR training through the City of Cleveland. On Martin Luther King Day 1988 I went to morning mass with Marge because I had a day off. Just after mass started, a teenage boy came rushing into the chapel yelling that his father was not breathing and needed help. I went tearing after him as did an off-duty fireman from our church. When we got to Jose he was a chalky beige color and he was not breathing as he lay on the floor. The fireman started chest massage as I started breathing air into his lungs. Within a minute he gurgled, gasped for air and began to breathe! Tests did not determine what had happened to Jose, but he was OK.

But there definitely was something that happened to me. I know I wouldn't have been at church that day if I had not been off work. I know I wouldn't have gone running with Jose's son had I not had the CPR training three months earlier. But this incident really shook me (and my feelings) up. I had trouble sleeping for several weeks after this happened. I felt awed that I could be an instrument of God to literally breathe life back into someone. I was scared because I could see myself lying on a floor, primarily because of my heart condition, being in need of resuscitation and being close to dying. And it brought back all those childhood memories and fears of abandonment as I would watch to see if my mother's chest was moving and that I could hear her breathing as she took a nap — I was so fearful that she would die and I would be without her. To me it was no coincidence that I learned CPR.

Reflecting on and adapting to my heart attack was the start of my recovery program in many ways. Considering mid-life crisis issues, being exposed to recovery principles through people like Joe and some of my clients, and episodes like helping Jose, culminated in my beginning to deal with my denial and with my co-dependency, in earnest, at the ripe old age of forty. Although it took several years, in January 1989 I ran out of excuses and set aside my fear and enrolled in an outpatient co-dependency recovery group at a local hospital.

Needless to say, my life has changed since then. From my upbringing as a child to the co-dependent roles I have played (controlling/people-pleasing) as a seminarian, step-parent, probation officer, and counselor, I feel that I have made considerable progress. Since that time I have been learning to identify and to express my feelings. I have been learning to take care of myself. I have been learning to be more confident, more trusting, and more loving. I have been learning and appreciating the fact that God loves me! And I have been learning that this recovery process is a necessary step for my personal well-being as well as for my Christian growth and spirituality. I have tried some things and taken some risks that I had never taken before. In some I have succeeded and in others I have not. I have been proud of the successes. But I have been less dejected or

disappointed with the failures than in the past because I know
that *who* I am is not being rejected, but rather *something* that
I have done has not worked out.

Since starting my recovery process, I have presented at a
state-wide seminar, written two articles that were published
in a national trade magazine in my field, been appointed supervisor at my job and written a book! Three of these four
I had never even thought of prior to beginning this process,
and I'm sure I would not have tried them had it not been for
my increased confidence and self-pride as well as a greater sense
of God's love and plan for me.

I had applied for a supervisory position at every opportunity for some six years without success. Basically I was praying for it because I wanted it for *me*. But then I began to pray
that God put me wherever *He* wanted me to be. In a process
that, in our court, often takes several weeks to several months
once the process begins, I was appointed supervisor within five
days of being interviewed! And I'm also convinced that it happened at that time because I was now more prepared to deal
with the pressures and the stress by virtue of the steps I was
taking in my recovery program. In my becoming me, God felt
that I was ready.

In my recovery, the more I have promoted myself and my
career with prayer and self care, the more God has blessed and
promoted me. Because, by turning my life over to God, there
is greater unity and harmony between my life and God's Will.
Certainly there are days when it still hurts, in which it seems
like a losing, uphill battle, and that it's taking "forever" —
looking at recovery as an event. But I recognize the fact that
I'm working on counteracting years of experince. But of this
I am certain: I am on the right track. My depression has les-
sened, the bouts are fewer and farther between times, I'm better
able to accept setbacks, and I feel better about myself and I'm
more "at home" with being me.

A last instance of grace that I would like to mention has
to do with my name, "Theodore." It comes from the Greek,
theou doron, meaning "gift of God." For years I have told

people jokingly what my name means followed by, "And don't you forget it!" But I didn't really appreciate it myself until four decades after it was given to me!

And it came up again when I made a Cursillo (it means, "the little way" — a weekend spiritual journey) recently. We were asked to write our names on our styrofoam cups in order to conserve. I decided to write the Polish translation of my name, "Tadeusz." I wrote it in big block letters. Sometime in the course of that day, I glanced at the cup and because of its contour all I could see was "DEUS," "God." God was in my name, "Ta-DEUS-z!" God was in me! As He is in all of us. It really blew me away to see that represented in a physical fashion. In many ways, I think that realization is the crux of this entire process for the co-dependent Christian. Because once I acknowledge that I am a gift from God, I can never go back, I will never be the same.

As I look back on this brief, episodic depiction of some of the highlights of my life, I can see the evolution, if you will, of God's revelation to me in my own life. From financial and material help through winning the $1,000 and the car, to physical help in that no one was injured in the car accident as well as my "natural bypass," to the emotional, psychological and spiritual planes of recovering from my heart attack, learning about co-dependency recovery, helping to save someone's life, to learning more about myself, my faith, about love and about hope.

The journey of faith might be summarized by the following short story:

Covenant

The Father knocked at my door seeking a home for his son:
"Rent is cheap," I say.
"I don't want to rent, I want to buy," says God.
"I'm not sure I want to sell, but you might come in to look around."

"I think I will," says God.

"I might let you have a room or two."

"I like it," says God. "I'll take the two. You might decide to give me more some day. I can wait," says God.

"I'd like to give you more, but it's a bit difficult. I need some space for me."

"I know," says God, "but I'll wait. I like what I see."

"Hm, maybe I can let you have another room. I really don't need that much."

"Thanks," says God. "I'll take it. I like what I see."

"I'd like to give you the whole house, but I'm not sure."

"Think on it," says God. "I wouldn't put you out. Your house would be mine and my son would live in it. You'd have more space than you'd ever had before."

"I don't understand at all."

"I know," says God, "but I can't tell you about that. You'll have to discover it yourself. That can only happen if you let him have the whole house."

"A bit risky," I say.

"Yes," says God, "but try me."

"I'm not sure — I'll let you know."

"I can wait," says God. "I like what I see."

— Sister Margaret Halasks, O.S.F. (citation unknown)

Similarly, the journey of co-dependency recovery may be summarized by this "autobiography":

Autobiography In Five Short Chapters
by
Portia Nelson

I.   I walk down the street.
There is a deep hole in the sidewalk.
I fall in.
I am lost . . . I am helpess.
It isn't my fault.
It takes forever to find a way out.

II.   I walk down the same street.
There is a deep hole in the sidewalk.

I pretend I don't see it.
I fall in again.

I can't believe I'm in the same place.
                    But it isn't my fault.
It still takes a long time to get out.

III.   I walk down the same street.
       There is a deep hole in the sidewalk.
       I see it is there.
       I still fall in . . . It's a habit.
                    My eyes are open.
                    I know where I am.
       It is my fault.
       I get out immediately.

IV.   I walk down the same street.
       There is a deep hole in the sidewalk.
       I walk around it.

V.   I walk down another street.

                              (citation unknown)

Armed with this insight into both our journey of faith and our journey of recovery, one last look at the Scriptures is in order. The person we want to visit is Peter, the Rock, the one to whom Jesus entrusted His Church. And the perspective that we want to take is that of Peter as a co-dependent follower of Jesus — a co-dependent Christian.

When we look at the co-dependency characteristics list, the basic behaviors that jump out are people-pleasing and controling or manipulating. There are at least four instances of Peter's attempting to control Jesus. Let us look at them.

The first occurs at Jesus' first prophecy of His Death and Resurrection: "At this, Peter took him aside and began to remonstrate with him. 'May you be spared, Master! God forbid that any such thing ever happen to you!' Jesus turned on Peter and said, 'Get out of my sight, you satan! You are trying to make me trip and fall. You are not judging by God's standards but by man's .' " (Matthew 16:22-23) Peter was trying to change what Jesus was struggling to understand for Himself. He did not need to hear His friend add to His confusion and pain concerning His impending death. It was difficult enough for Him to face this possibility.

The second occurs at the transfiguration: "About eight days after saying this he took Peter, John and James, and went up onto a mountain to pray. While he was praying, his face changed in appearance and his clothes became dazzlingly white. Suddenly two men were talking with him — Moses and Elijah. They appeared in glory and spoke of his passage, which he was about to fulfill in Jerusalem. Peter and those with him had fallen into a deep sleep; but awakening, they saw his glory and likewise saw the two men who were standing with him. When these were leaving, Peter said to Jesus, 'Master, how good it is for us to be here. Let us set up three booths, one for you, one for Moses, and one for Elijah.' (He did not really know what he was saying.) While he was speaking, a cloud came and overshadowed them, and the disciples grew fearful as the others entered it. Then from the cloud came a voice which said, 'This is my Son, my Chosen One. Listen to him.' When the voice fell silent, Jesus was there alone. The disciples kept quiet, telling nothing of what they had seen at that time to anyone." (Luke 9:28-36)

Peter is alluding to the Jewish Feast of Tabernacles which commemorates Moses receiving the commandments, the Law, on Mount Sinai, when he talks about setting up three tents. "But this is not the revelation of another Law; a greater reality is manifested here."[3] Peter is both missing and minimizing the significance of this event for Jesus and for the disciples, thus possibly clouding Jesus' awareness of His mission and His identity.

When Jesus was arrested, Peter did it again. "Then Simon Peter, who had a sword, drew it and struck the slave of the high priest, severing his right ear . . . . At that Jesus said to

Peter, 'Put your sword back in its sheath. Am I not to drink the cup the Father has given me?' '' (John 18:10-11) As He says later at His "trial" before Pilate, His kingdom is not of this world, so fighting would not do. But Peter tried it anyway.

Lastly, in Jesus' appearance in Galilee after the Resurrection, we see a pushy, controlling Peter put in his place once again: "Peter turned around at that, and noticed that the disciple whom Jesus loved was following . . . . Seeing him, Peter was prompted to ask Jesus, 'But Lord, what about him?' 'Suppose I want him to stay until I come,' Jesus replied, 'How does that concern you? Your business is to follow me.' '' (John 21:20-22)

Another characteristic of a co-dependent person is the inability to trust. This is manifest in Peter at the time that Jesus walked on the water: "When the disciples saw him walking on the water, they were terrified. 'It is a ghost!' they said, and in their fear they began to cry out. Jesus hastened to reassure them: 'Get hold of yourselves! It is I. Do not be afraid!' Peter spoke up and said, 'Lord, if it is really you, tell me to come to you across the water.' 'Come!' he said. So Peter got out of the boat and began to walk on the water, moving toward Jesus. But when he perceived how strong the wind was, becoming frightened, he began to sink and cried out, 'Lord, save me!' Jesus at once stretched out his hand and caught him. 'How little faith you have!' he exclaimed. 'Why did you falter?' Once they had climbed into the boat, the wind died down.'' (Matthew 14:26-32) Despite all the miracles that Peter had seen Jesus create, when it came down to his being personally involved, Peter found it difficult to trust Jesus.

A further example of co-dependent behavior is found in the "people-pleasing" (in this case Peter attempting to please Jesus by saying the "right" thing) and the extremes or over reacting on Peter's part. An example of the "Jesus pleasing" is found in Jesus' washing of the feet of the disciples. "Then he poured water into a basin and began to wash his disciples' feet and dry them with the towel he had around him. Thus he came to Simon Peter, who said to him, 'Lord, are you going to wash my feet?' Jesus answered, 'You may not realize now what I am doing, but later you will understand.' Peter replied, 'You shall never wash my feet!' 'If I do not wash you,' Jesus answered, 'you will have no share in my heritage.' 'Lord,' Simon Peter said to him, 'then not only my feet, but my hands and head as well.' '' (John 13:5-9) At first it was OK for Jesus to wash the others' feet, but not Peter's. *Never!* But when he heard Jesus' reply, Peter went to the other extreme and wanted Jesus to wash more than just his feet!

The second instance of extremist behavior — devoid of the middle ground — is found in Peter's statements before and after Jesus' arrest. Before the arrest, Peter said he would lay down his life for Jesus (John 13:37), but after His arrest, not only did Peter not lay down his life for Jesus, but he denied even knowing Jesus! (Matthew 26:72)

This is the man that Jesus chose to be the head of His Church, the Rock! (And Jesus did not change His mind.) Peter seemed to be verbally and theologically ''clumsy,'' he seemed to botch things, and sometimes he had not one, but both feet in his mouth. It makes one wonder if Jesus might not have been better off if He had had a search committee!

What was it that Jesus saw in Peter? If it is true, as some suggest, that most of us use only ten percent of our potential, Jesus saw the other ninety percent! He saw the butterfly. He saw the passion, the possibility, the love, the leadership, and the faith. For in all of his humanity, it was Peter who acknowledged Jesus as the Messiah, ''the Son of the living God.'' (Matthew 16:15) And in all of his humanity, his passion for life, his co-dependency, his faults and his strengths, Peter was chosen by Jesus to lead His Church. Therefore, there is certainly hope for each of us as we struggle to lead a Christ-like life and learn to overcome our co-dependency.

A good motto seems to be the Serenity Prayer because it is short, all-inclusive, and to the point:

God, grant me the serenity to accept the things I cannot change, the courage to change the things that I can, and the wisdom to know the difference. Help me to live one day at a time, enjoying one moment at a time, accepting hardship as a pathway to peace, taking, as your Son, Jesus did, this sinful world as it is, not as I would have it, trusting that You will make all things right if I surrender to Your will so that I may be reasonably happy in this life and supremely happy with You forever in the next. Amen.

— Reinhold Niebuhr

Added to that is Fr. John Powell, S. J.'s statement that what I *am* is God's gift to me; what I *become* is my gift to God.[4]

Life provides us with many opportunities to make new beginnings: a new year, a new season, a birthday, an anniversary, a significant event. Starting a co-dependency recovery process in a Christian perspective can be just such an opportunity. Muster your courage. Open your heart. Look to your faith. It is not a journey of distance or space. Rather it is a journey of time and grace. Why not begin? "Don't run, go slowly, for it's only to yourself that you have to go."

How does this book help you relate to the "Big Picture" of life?

How can these changes and this process help you impact your environment — people, places and things?

Are there instances of seredipity in your life? Give examples.

What are some "grace moments" in your life?

Recall a time in your life when "a door was closed but a window was opened."

Can you relate to Peter as a co-dependent?

Name three things that you would like to accomplish with the rest of your life.

Recount a spiritual experience in which you felt "God's hand on your shoulder."

Endnotes

Foreword

[1]Fr. John F. Loya, *Gfits From the Poor* (Nashville, Tennessee: Winston-Derek Publishers, Inc., 1990), p. 11.

Introduction

[1]Melody Beattie, *Codependent No More* (Center City, Minnesota: Hazelden, 1987), Front Cover.

[2]Lynda Spann and Judith Fischer, "Identifying Codependency" *The Counselor*, VIII (March-April 1990), p. 27.

Chapter I

[1]Adaption by Issac Watts, 1674-1748. Music: William Craft, 1678-1727. *Breaking Bread Hymnal* (Portland, Oregon: Oregon Catholic Press, 1967), No. 261.

Chapter II

[1]Text Based on Ps. 46; Martin Luther, *Breaking Bread Hymnal* (Portland, Oregon: Oregon Catholic Press, 1992), No. 329.

[2]Rev. John Powell, S. J., *Through Seasons of the Heart* (Allen, Texas: Tabor Publishing, 1967), p. 9.

[3]Ibid. p. 20.

[4]Rev. Martin Padovani, *Healing Memories and Forgiveness* (video) [Complete citation unknown]

[5]Powell, op. cit., p. 122.

[6] Claudia Black, *Children of Denial* (video) (Center City, Minnesota: Hazelden)

[7]Rev. Joseph Gallagher, *The Christian Under Pressure* (Notre Dame, Indiana: Ave Maria Press, 1970), p. 95.

[8]Earnie Larsen, *Stage II Recovery: Life After Addiction* (audio tape) E. Larsen Enterprises, Inc. available through Hazelden Publications, Center City, Minnesota.

Chapter III

[1]Sebastian Temple, *Breaking Bread Hymnal* (Portland, Oregon: Oregon Catholic Press, 1967), No. 353.

[2]Melody Beattie, *Codependent No More* (Center City, Minnesota: Hazelden, 1987) p. 91.

[3]M. Scott Peck, M.D., *The Road Less Traveled* (New York: Simon & Schuster, 1978), p. 81.

[4]Beattie, *op. cit.*, p. 86.

[5]Rev. Joseph Gallagher, *The Christian Under Pressure* (Notre Dame, Indiana: Ave Maria Press, 1970), p. 42.

[6]Beattie, *op. cit.*, p. 86.

[7]Gallagher, *op. cit.*, p. 73.

Chapter IV

[1]Linda Creed and Michael Masser © 1977 by Gold Horizon Music Corp., A Division of Filmtrax Copyright Holdings Inc. and Golden Torch Music Corp., A Division of Filmtrax Copyright Holdings, Inc. All rights reserved.

[2]Rev. Joseph Gallagher, *The Christian Under Pressure* (Notre Dame, Indiana: Ave Maria Press, 1970), p. 28.

[3]Raymond E. Brown, S.S. et al. (ed.), *The Jerome Biblical Commentary* (Englewood Cliffs, New Jersey: Prentice-Hall, Inc., 1968), p. 108.

[4]Ibid., p. 782.

[5]Ibid., p. 93.

[6]M. Scott Peck, M.D., *The Road Less Traveled* (New York: Simon & Schuster, 1978), p. 35.

[7]Gallagher, *op. cit.*, pp. 66-68.

[8]Rev. John Powell, S. J., *Happiness Is an Inside Job*, (Allen, Texas: Tabor Publishing, 1989), p. 15.

[9]Rev. John Powell, S. J., *Through Seasons of the Heart* (Allen, Texas: Tabor Publishing, 1987), p. 23.

[10]Gallagher, *op. cit.*, pp. 34-35.

[11]Powell, *Happiness Is an Inside Job, op. cit.*, p. 47.

[12]Joe S., *Out Of Hell: (An Adult Child of an Alcoholic/Dysfunctional Family Recovery Saga)* (Lakewood, Ohio: State of the Art Publishing, 1991), p. 112.

[13]Gallagher, *op. cit.*, p. 29.

[14]Joe S., *op. cit.*, p. 290.

[15]Ibid., p. 98.

[16]Gallagher, *op. cit.*, p. 24.

[17]Ibid., p. 105.

[18]Melody Beattie, *Codependent No More* (Center City, Minnesota: Hazelden, 1987), p. 113.

[19]Gallagher, *op. cit.*, p. 15.

[20]Beattie, *op. cit.*, p. 92.

Chapter V

[1]Sy Miller and Jill Jackson, *Breaking Bread Hymnal* (Portland, Oregon: Oregon Catholic Press, 1955), No. 405.

[2]Rev. John Powell, S. J., *Through Seasons of the Heart* (Allen, Texas: Tabor Publishing, 1987), p. 201.

[3]Rev. Joseph Gallagher, *The Christian Under Pressure* (Notre Dame, Indiana: Ave Maria Press, 1970), p. 62.

[4]Melody Beattie, *Codependent No More* (Center City, Minnesota: Hazelden, 1987), p. 116.

[5]M. Scott Peck, M.D., *The Road Less Traveled* (New York: Simon & Schuster, 1978), p. 260.

[6]Ibid., p. 308.

[7]Beattie, *op. cit.*, p. 121.

Conclusion

[1]John Newton and Virginia Harmony, *Breaking Bread Hymnal* (Portland, Oregon: Oregon Catholic Press, 1989), No. 387.

[2]Rev. John Powell, S. J., *Happiness Is an Inside Job* (Allen, Texas: Tabor Publishing, 1989), p. 85.

[3]Raymond E. Brown, S.S. et. al (ed.), *The Jerome Biblical Commentary* (Englewood Cliffs, New Jersey: Prentice-Hall, Inc., 1968), p. 93.

[4]Rev. John Powell, S.J., *Through Seasons of the Heart* (Allen, Texas: Tabor Publishing, 1987), p. 376.

Appendix I
Co-dependency Characteristics/ Profile Of A Child Of An Alcoholic Or Other Dysfunctional Family System

We become isolated, afraid and/or defiant of others, especially authority figures.

We become approval seekers and lose some of our identity in the process.

We are frightened by angry people and any personal criticism, and react by either fight or flight.

We either become alcoholics, marry them, or both, or find compulsive personalities such as workaholics to fulfill our unconscious need for abandonment.

We live life from the viewpoint of victims and are attracted by that weakness in our love, friendship and career relationships.

We have an overdeveloped sense of responsibility and it is easier for us to be concerned with others rather than ourselves; this enables us not to look too closely at our faults or our responsibilities to ourselves. We take what we do too seriously.

We sometimes feel guilty or angry when we stand up for ourselves, so we give in to others.

We become addicted to excitement, although we have difficulty having fun.

We have difficulty with intimacy, confuse love and pity, and tend to "love" people we can pity and rescue.

We have stuffed many of our feelings from our childhood and have lost some of the ability to feel or express our feelings today because it hurts too much. This includes our good feelings such as joy and happiness. Being out of touch with our feelings is one of our basic denials.

We judge ourselves harshly and have a low sense of self-esteem.

We are dependent personalities who are afraid of abandonment and will often do almost anything to hold onto a relationship in order to avoid painful abandonment feelings which we received from living with unhealthy people who were never there for us.

We are either super responsible or super irresponsible, but in each we tend to be impulsive, looking for immediate rather than delayed gratification of needs or goals.

We take on the characteristics of the disease of alcoholism even though we may never have picked up a drink.

We are reactors rather than actors, often over-reacting to things which are often beyond our control.

We are loyal even in the face of proof that our loyalty is un-derserved.

We guess at what is normal.

We have difficulty following a project through from beginning to end.

We tend to continually seek approval and affirmation and when affirmation is offered, it is difficult to accept.

We sometimes feel different from other people. We become isolated as a result, with socializing becoming increasingly difficult.

We are compulsive about certain things, like work, relationships, hobbies, etc.

We sometimes lie even though it would be easier to tell the
truth.

Control Patterns

We must be ''needed'' in order to have a relationship with
others.

We value others' approval of our thinking, feelings, and behaviors over our own.

We agree with others so they will like us.

We focus our attention on protecting others.

We believe most people are incapable of taking care of themselves.

We keep score of ''good deeds and favors'' and become hurt
when they are not repaid.

We are skilled at guessing how other people are feeling.

We can anticipate others' needs, meeting them before they are
asked to be met.

We become resentful when others will not let us help them.

We are calm and efficient in other people's crisis situations.

We put aside our own interests and concerns in order to do
what others want.

We ask for help and nurturing only when we're ill, and then
reluctantly.

We cannot tolerate seeing others in pain.

We lavish gifts and favors on those we care about.

We use sex to gain approval and acceptance.

We attempt to convince others of how they ''truly'' think and
''should'' feel.

We perceive ourselves as completely unselfish and dedicated
to the well-being of others.

Compliance Patterns

We assume responsibility for others' feelings and behaviors.

We feel guilty about others' feelings and behaviors.

We are afraid of our anger, yet sometimes erupt in a rage.

We have difficulty making decisions.

We are afraid of being hurt and/or rejected by others.

We are sensitive to how others are feeling and feel the same.

We are afraid to express differing opinions or feelings.

We are embarrassed to receive recognition and praise, or gifts.

We judge everything we think, say or do harshly, as never
"good enough."

We are perfectionistic.

We do not ask others to meet our needs or desires.

We do not perceive ourselves as lovable or worthwhile persons.

We compromise our own values and integrity to avoid rejection.

Being able to relate to any number of these characteristics in
various combinations would constitute co-dependency, and it
would be worthwhile for you to pursue this further.

(These characertistics and patterns are a composite gathered
from various sources.)

Ten Commandments

I. I am the Lord your God, you shall not have false gods before Me.

II. You shall not take the name of the Lord your God in vain.

III. Remember to keep holy the Lord's day.

IV. Honor your father and your mother.

V. You shall not kill.

VI. You shall not commit adultery.

VII. You shall not steal.

VIII. You shall not give false witness against your neighbor.

IX. You shall not covet your neighbor's wife.

X. You shall not covet your neighbor's property.

(Based on the Decalogue in Deuteronomy 5:6-21)

The Beatitudes

Blessed are the poor in spirit; the reign of God is theirs.

Blessed are the sorrowing; they shall be consoled.

Blessed are the lowly; they shall inherit the land.

Blessed are they who hunger and thirst for holiness; they shall have their fill.

Blessed are they who show mercy; mercy shall be theirs.

Blessed are the single-hearted for they shall see God.

Blessed are the peacemakers; they shall be called sons of God.

Blessed are those persecuted for holiness' sake; the reign of
God is theirs.

Blessed are you when they insult you and persecute you and
utter every kind of slander against you because of me.
Be glad and rejoice, for your reward is great in heaven;
they persecuted the prophets before you in the very same
way. (Based on Matthew 5:3-12)

Appendix III
Dysfunctional Family Childhood Roles

I. The Lost Child

While acting withdrawn and aloof from general family activities, the lost child is quiet, distant and very independent. This child often rejects others. The inner feelings are loneliness, inadequacy, being hurt and anger. The child does not want to get involved in the mainstream of family life in order to avoid the situation. The child will spend a lot of time alone. This child wants to be "good."

II. The Mascot

This child is the family clown who is super cute, uses humor to ease family tension, and basically does anything to attract attention in order to take the focus off the real problem. The child can be hyperactive and fragile. The child's feelings are fear, insecurity, confusion and loneliness. This child wants to be a distraction.

III. The Family Hero

Motivated by success and an attempt to have a strong sense of self-worth, this child is super responsible, special, works hard to get approval and acceptance, seems to have it "all together," and develops an independent life away from the family. This is often the oldest in the family. The inner feelings are hurt, loneliness, inadequacy, confusion and anger, despite the facade.

IV. The Scapegoat.

This is the problem child and the one who gets the negative attention by getting into trouble. The child is withdrawn, defiant, acts out (which can be drug usage, an unwanted pregnancy, poor grades, etc.), and has strong peer values. This child feels alone, anger, hurt, fear and rejection.

Note the similarity in feelings of all four children despite the different family roles. Also, note that in reality we may play different roles at different times, but usually one or two seem to dominate. In addition, an only child may play all four roles throughout childhood.

(This is based on a model developed by Sharon Wegscheider-Cruse.)

A Comparison Of Non-Assertive, Assertive, And Aggressive Behavior

	Non-Assertive	Assertive	Aggressive
Characteristics of the Behavior:	Does not express wants, ideas, and feelings, or expresses them in a self-depreciating way.	Expresses wants, ideas, and feelings in direct and appropriate ways.	Expresses wants, ideas, and feelings at the expense of others
	Intent: to please	Intent: to communicate	Intent: to dominate or humiliate
Your Feelings When Act this Way:	Anxious, disappointed with yourself. Often angry & resentful later.	Confident, feel good about yourself at the time and later.	Self-righteous, superior. Sometimes embarrassed later.
Other People's Feelings About Themselves When You Act This Way:	Guilty or Superior.	Respected, Valued	Humiliated, Hurt.
Other People's Feelings About You When You Act This Way:	Irritated, Pity Disgusted	Usually Respect	Angry, Vengeful
Outcome:	Don't get what you want. Anger builds up.	Often get what you want	Often get what you want at the expense of others. Others feel justified at "getting even."
Pay-off:	Avoids unpleasant situation, avoids conflict, tension, confrontation.	Feels good, respected by others. Improved self-confidence, Relationships are improved.	Vents anger, feels superior.

153

Assertive Behavior

Assertive behavior enables a person to act in his or her own best interests, to stand up for herself or himself without undue anxiety, to express honest feelings comfortably, or to exercise personal rights without denying the rights of others.

To act in one's own best interests refers to the ability to make life decisions, (career, relationships, life style, time schedule), to take initiative (start conversations, organize activities), to trust one's own judgment, to set goals and work to achieve them, to ask help from others, to participate socially.

To stand up for oneself includes such behaviors as saying "no," setting limits on time and energy, responding to criticism or put-downs or anger, expressing or supporting or defending an opinion.

To express honest feelings comfortably means the ability to disagree, to show anger, to show affection or friendship, to admit fear or anxiety, to express agreement or support, to be spontaneous — all without painful anxiety.

To exercise personal rights relates to competency (as a citizen, as a consumer, as a member of an organization or school or work group, as a participant in public events) to express opinions, to work for change, to respond to violations of one's own rights or those of others.

To deny the rights of others is to accomplish the above personal expressions without unfair criticism of others, without hurtful behavior toward others, without name-calling, without intimidation, without manipulation, without controlling others.

Thus, assertive behavior is a positive self-affirmation which also values the other people in your life. It contributes both to your personal life satisfaction and to the quality of your relationships with others.

Some Assertive Rights

1. You have the right and responsibility to control your own life.

2. You have the right to hold and express your own feelings, thoughts, and opinions and to be your own judge.

3. You have the right to be treated with respect and to be taken seriously.

4. You have the right to err and to change your mind.

5. You have the right to be human (not perfect) and not to be liked by everyone.

6. You have the right to make and refuse requests without feeling guilty.

7. You have the right to get what you pay for.

8. You have the right to choose not to pursue a personal right.

Appendix IV used with permission, Kaiser Permanente Health Education Division, 1992.

Appendix V

The 12 Steps Of Recovery

1. We admitted we were powerless over the effects of alcoholism and other dysfunction, and that our lives had become unmanageable.

2. Came to believe that a power greater than ourselves could restore us to sanity.

3. Made a decision to turn our will and our lives over to the care of God, *as we understood God.*

4. Made a searching and fearless moral inventory of ourselves.

5. Admitted to God, to ourselves, and to another human being the exact nature of our wrongs.

6. Were entirely ready to have God remove all these defects of character.

7. Humbly asked God to remove our shortcomings.

8. Made a list of all persons we had harmed, and became willing to make amends to them all.

9. Made direct amends to such people whenever possible, except when to do so would injure them or others.

10. Continued to take personal inventory and when we were wrong promptly admitted it.

11. Sought through prayer and meditation to improve our conscious contact with God *as we understood God*, praying only for knowledge of God's will for us and the power to carry that out.

12. Having had a spiritual awakening as the result of these steps, we tried to carry this message to Adult Children of Alcoholics and other Dysfunctions, and to practice these principles in all our affairs.

The Twelve Steps
Of Alcoholics Anonymous

1. We admitted we were powerless over alcohol — that our lives had become unmanagable.

2. Came to believe a Power greater than ourselves could restore us to sanity.

3. Made a decision to turn our will and our lives over to the care of God *as we understood Him.*

4. Made a searching and fearless moral inventory of ourselves.

5. Admitted to God, to ourselves and to another human being the exact nature of our wrongs.

6. Were entirely ready to have God remove all these defects of character.

7. Humbly asked Him to remove our shortcomings.

8. Made a list of all persons we had harmed, and became willing to make amends to them all.

9. Made direct amends to such people wherever possible, except when to do so would injure them or others.

10. Continued to take personal inventory and when we were wrong promptly admitted it.

11. Sought through prayer and meditation to improve our conscious contact with God, *as we understood Him*, praying only for knowledge of His will for us and the power to carry that out.

12. Having had a spiritual awakening as the result of these steps, we tried to carry this message to alcoholics, and to practice these principles in all our affairs.

Permissions

For "The Prayer of St. Francis" at the beginning of Chapter III: "Dedicated to Mrs. Frances Tracy," reprinted with permission, Franciscan Communications, Los Angeles, CA. © 1967.

Permission for "Greatest Love Of All" at the beginning of Chapter IV by Linda Creed and Michael Masser. Copyright © 1977 by Gold Horizon Music Corp., a division of Filmtrax Copyright Holdings, Inc. and Golden Touch Music Corp., a division of Filmtrax Copyright Holdings Inc. All rights reserved. Made in U.S.A. International copyright secured. Used by permission of CPP/Belwin, Inc. P.O. Box 4340 Miami, FL 33014.

For Appendix IV regarding Assertive/Non-Assertive/Aggressive Behavior. "Used with permission, Kaiser Permanente Health Education Division, 1992."